CONDITIONING AND INSTRUMENTAL LEARNING

BASIC CONCEPTS IN PSYCHOLOGY SERIES

Edward L. Walker, Editor

GENERAL

PSYCHOLOGY AS A NATURAL AND SOCIAL SCIENCE	Edward L. Walker
TEACHING THE BEGINNING COURSE IN PSYCHOLOGY	Edward L. Walker and Wilbert J. McKeachie
A LABORATORY MANUAL FOR THE CONTROL AND ANALYSIS OF BEHAVIOR	Harlan L. Lane and Daryl J. Bem
QUANTIFICATION IN PSYCHOLOGY	William L. Hays
BASIC STATISTICS	William L. Hays

PSYCHOLOGY: A NATURAL SCIENCE

NEUROPSYCHOLOGY: THE STUDY OF BRAIN AND BEHAVIOR	Charles M. Butter
SENSORY PROCESSES	Mathew Alpern, Merle Lawrence, and David Wolsk
PERCEPTION	Daniel J. Weintraub and Edward L. Walker
HUMAN PERFORMANCE	Paul M. Fitts and Michael I. Posner
CONDITIONING AND INSTRUMENTAL LEARNING	Edward L. Walker

PSYCHOLOGY: A SOCIAL SCIENCE

MOTIVATION: A STUDY OF ACTION	David Birch and Joseph Veroff
THE CONCEPT OF HUMAN DEVELOPMENT	Elton B. McNeil
PSYCHODYNAMICS: THE SCIENCE OF UNCONSCIOUS MENTAL FORCES	Gerald S. Blum
ASSESSMENT OF HUMAN CHARACTERISTICS	E. Lowell Kelly
COGNITIVE PROCESSES	Melvin Manis
SOCIAL PSYCHOLOGY: AN EXPERIMENTAL APPROACH	Robert B. Zajonc
NON-FREUDIAN PERSONALITY THEORIES	P. James Geiwitz
BELIEFS, ATTITUDES, AND HUMAN AFFAIRS	Daryl J. Bem
CLINICAL PSYCHOLOGY: AN EMPIRICAL APPROACH	Erasmus L. Hoch
ABNORMAL PSYCHOLOGY	James Neal Butcher

BROOKS/COLE PUBLISHING COMPANY
A Division of Wadsworth Publishing Company, Inc., Belmont, California

CONDITIONING AND INSTRUMENTAL LEARNING

EDWARD L. WALKER

The University of Michigan

BROOKS/COLE PUBLISHING COMPANY
Belmont, California

A Division of Wadsworth Publishing Company, Inc.

To Alice and Bruce

5 6 7 8 9 10—74 73 72

L. C. Cat. Card No.: 67-17555

Printed in the United States of America

SERIES FOREWORD

Basic Concepts in Psychology was conceived as a series of brief paperback volumes constituting a beginning textbook in psychology. Several unique advantages arise from publishing individual chapters as separate volumes rather than under a single cover. Each book or chapter can be written by an author identified with the subject matter of the area. New chapters can be added, individual chapters can be revised independently, and, possibly, competitive chapters can be provided for controversial areas. Finally, to a degree, an instructor of the beginning course in psychology can choose a particular set of chapters to meet the needs of his students.

Probably the most important impetus for the series came from the fact that a suitable textbook did not exist for the beginning courses in psychology at the University of Michigan—Psychology 100 (Psychology as a Natural Science) and Psychology 101 (Psychology as a Social Science). In addition, no laboratory manual treated both the natural science and social science problems encountered in the first laboratory course, Psychology 110.

For practical rather than ideological reasons most of the original complement of authors came from the staff of the University of Michigan. As the series has developed, authors have been selected from other institutions in an effort to assure national representation and a broad perspective in contemporary psychology.

Each author in the Basic Concepts in Psychology Series has considerable freedom. He has been charged to devote approximately half of his resources to elementary concepts and half to topics of special interest and emphasis. In this way, each volume will reflect the personality and viewpoint of the author while presenting the subject matter usually found in a chapter of an elementary textbook.

ACKNOWLEDGMENTS

I wish to gratefully acknowledge the helpful comments of Professors James A. Dyal, F. Joseph Mortenson, and Jon L. Williams, who read the entire manuscript. And for their advice on portions of the manuscript, I thank Professors J. David Birch, Harlan L. Lane, Walter R. Reitman, and Robert B. Zajonc.

CONTENTS

The sea contains many small organisms that have little or no capacity as individuals to adjust to minor changes in the environment. The metabolism of these passively floating organisms depends directly on a narrow range of temperature and chemical conditions. Their survival through the ages has depended on variation among individuals—those best suited to slight environmental changes have survived; those least suited have perished.

As one proceeds up the phylogenetic scale, the capacity to behave increases, and the behavior available to the organism in adjusting to his environment becomes more complex. The behavior of some species, although complex, remains rigid and stereotyped. Such behavior is referred to as instinctive—little capacity to learn is in evidence, and there is great dependence on a particular environmental pattern. In other species, there appears to be more capacity to vary behavior in response to environmental change, more capacity for learning, and a wider range of environments in which an individual can survive. Thus variability in the individual's behavior—and individual survival under changing circumstances—becomes an important mechanism in the survival of the species.

Man can live and thrive in most of the environments on earth and is less subject than most species to extinction by gradual changes in the environment. Of all living creatures, he seems to acquire the greatest store of information, to develop the greatest repertory of motor skills, and to modify his behavior, through learning, to meet the greatest range of situations. There seems to be an evolutionary process in which men with the greatest ability to learn and to vary their behavior survive at the expense of those with less flexible behavior and less learning capacity.

WHAT IS LEARNING?

Let us say tentatively that learning is *a change in performance that occurs as a result of experience*. This short and simple statement appears to include everything that one would want in a definition of learning.

It clearly implies the concept of variability—variability is a prerequisite to any change in performance. Furthermore, we used the phrase "change in performance" in contrast to the more commonly used "improvement in performance" since one can acquire bad habits as well as good ones. The word "improvement" would eliminate many interesting problems from the study of learning.

The major difficulty with this simple definition is that there are times when we can attribute "changes in performance that occur as a result of experience" to factors other than learning. Before attempting a more precise definition of learning, we should consider some of these factors—maturation, fatigue, motivation, and changes in the stimulus situation.

STIMULUS-INDUCED MATURATION

The concept of *maturation* usually implies the appearance of capacities or behaviors that are due to the nature of an organism and not to its experience. For example, newborn puppies come into the world with closed eyes, as do the newborn of many other species. When a pup's eyes become fully open as he matures, his behavior changes. There is little doubt that this change in behavior is the result of maturation—not of experience or learning. On the other hand, maturation itself sometimes seems to be a product of stimulation. Riesen (1950) has shown that young chimpanzees reared through an early critical stage of their lives without experiencing light do not develop properly—their vision is irreparably damaged. Thus, in certain instances, the distinction between maturation and learning is far from clear cut. Moreover, we do not yet know exactly which aspects of development can be attributed to maturation and which require stimulation and thus can be attributed to learning. The history of psychology records many lengthy debates, none of which has produced a clear answer. Another volume in this series (McNeil, *The Concept of Human Development*, 1966) emphasizes maturation in the context of normal development, while the present volume is concerned with acquired behavior in which maturation plays less of a role. Our definition of learning will exclude behavior that results from normal maturation.

FATIGUE

Practice makes perfect; it also makes one tired. Although fatigue can produce "a change in performance that occurs as a result of experience," we do not consider such a change to be learned. The exhausted behavior of the tired runner disappears with rest, and his former swiftness is recovered. Learned behavior is more permanent. Thus we can use the relative permanence of behavioral changes to distinguish between learning and fatigue.

MOTIVATIONAL CHANGES

We also want to distinguish between motivation and learning. Learned acts are usually performed well only when one is motivated to perform them; and practice can sometimes produce changes in motivation that result in changes in performance. Such changes, however, are not the result of learning. For example, suppose we want to have a rat learn the shortest path from the start to the goal of a complicated maze. To make sure that the animal will be motivated to learn, we deprive him of food for a day and use food as a reward by placing it in the goal box. Each time the rat reaches the goal box, we allow him to eat for a while and then we place him back in the starting box. For a number of trials, the animal's performance keeps improving. He runs faster each time and makes fewer errors. But then he begins to run more slowly, to wander around in blind alleys; eventually he does not run at all but curls up and goes to sleep somewhere in the maze. He has, we think, no further interest in getting to the goal box for more food. His behavior has changed, and the change has occurred as a result of experience—but was the change due to motivation rather than learning? We can deprive him of food for a second day and then place him back in the maze. If he runs rapidly to the goal with few errors, we can be relatively sure that the performance change near the end of the first day was the result of a change in motivation. We do not wish to attribute such a change to learning.

CHANGES IN THE STIMULUS SITUATION

By learning, we mean some change that occurs inside the organism, probably in the nervous system. In laboratory studies of learning, an effort is made to keep the stimulus environment constant during the learning process, so that changes in behavior can be identified as changes in the organism and not in the external stimulus. In many ordinary situations in which learning occurs, what an organism does changes the environment. Such a change may in turn cause a new mode of behavior to appear. We do not wish to describe such behavior as learned—even though it might occur as the result of practice or experience.

This list of experiential factors that we wish to exclude from our definition of learning is already long, but is not exhaustive. The list should be left open to accommodate future developments. With this in mind, we revise our definition of learning:

Learning is a change in performance that occurs as a result of experience and is not attributable to maturation, fatigue, motivation, changes in the stimulus situation, or to other identifiable nonlearning factors.

THE CLASSES OF LEARNING

Because of its diversity, we choose to divide the realm of learning into three sub-areas: the learning of skills, the learning of facts, and the transfer of responses.[1]

This volume deals with the third area of learning, which is primarily concerned with the transfer of a response from one stimulus to another, the selection of one response from a set of responses which occur naturally in a situation, and changes in rate of emission or performance of responses. We will treat these problems in order of the amount of variability involved. Thus we will begin with *instinctive behavior,* in which stereotypy and rigidity are characteristic and in which learning is probably a negligible factor. Then we will take up imprinting, which involves complex patterns of behavior that can be linked to a wide variety of stimuli. Imprinting represents a slight increase in variability and introduces something like learning. Next, early-experience research illustrates the dependence of later learning on early learning. *Classical conditioning* (Chapters 3 and 4) involves more flexibility in both stimuli and responses. In conditioning, true learning occurs, but the requisite variability is at a minimum. *Instrumental learning* (also discussed in Chapters 3 and 4) involves even more flexibility in behavior and is based on reward or reinforcement. With *operant conditioning* (Chapter 5), a special form of selective learning, and *imitation and modeling* (Chapter 6), we will reach a maximum of flexibility in behavior.

The final chapter is a brief introduction to mathematic models, which are of increasing importance in learning theory, and in which the full range of variability can be represented.

---

[1] The learning of skills, especially motor skills, is referred to as *perceptual-motor learning.* The phenomena of perceptual-motor learning can be and often are treated almost independently of other kinds of learning. Separate treatment is given to the learning of perceptual-motor skills in another volume in this series (Fitts and Posner, *Human Performance,* 1967). Similarly, human information processing and human verbal learning are treated separately, as in this series (see Manis, *Cognitive Processes,* 1966).

A minimum of behavioral variability and, consequently, a minimum role for learning is evident in the three classes of behavior to be considered in this chapter. The classes are instinctive behavior, imprinting, and early experience (of certain kinds).

INSTINCTIVE BEHAVIOR

The term *instinctive* refers to complex behavior that appears to develop without the benefit of learning from prior experience. Instinctive behavior is usually stereotyped and thus not ordinarily modified through learning.

The sex life of the three-spined stickleback (*gasterosteus aculeatus*) as described by Tinbergen (1952) is a good illustration of instinctive behavior. The stickleback is a small, common fish found in the shallow streams, canals, and ditches of Europe. Tinbergen (1951) distinguished four large sequential segments of the reproductive behavior of the male stickleback. In the spring (1) the male establishes a territory and fights with other male sticklebacks. (2) He then builds a nest, and (3) he begins courting and mating behavior. Finally, (4) he develops a brood. Each of these four major phases consists of chains of simpler segments of behavior, each initiated and controlled by a limited set of highly specific external stimuli, called *sign stimuli* by Tinbergen.

The fighting behavior of the stickleback is directed almost exclusively toward other males with nuptial markings. Since the throat and belly of the male turns red during the mating season, Pelkwijk and Tinbergen (1937) suspected that the red color was the important stimulus that elicits fighting behavior. To test their hypothesis they constructed models of sticklebacks (see Figure 2.1). Some models (Series N) were shaped like sticklebacks but were silver and green with no red. Another set of models (Series R) lacked many of the figural characteristics of sticklebacks or even fish, but they had a red underside. When both kinds of models were presented to the male stickleback, he attacked those with red undersides more vigorously than the more accurately formed silver-and-green models. In one report, Tinbergen (1952) relates that a red mail truck driving past the window at a distance of more than 100 yards could induce the male to attack the side of the tank vigorously.

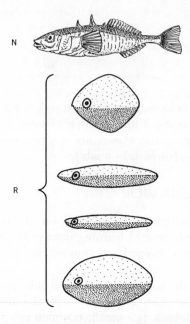

Figure 2.1

Models used in tests of fighting behavior in the three-spined stickleback. The heavily stippled lower portion of the models in series R is red. (Adapted from N. Tinbergen, The Study of Instinct, 1951 [Clarendon Press, Oxford], by permission.)

It is obvious that the stickleback was able to perceive the realistic silver-and-green model but that his instinctive fighting behavior was elicited only by red coloration. Limited sets of stimuli which elicit complex instinctive behavior are called *sign stimuli*. Since the stickleback's fighting behavior is elicited only by sign stimuli, and only when the stickleback is in an appropriate physiological state signaled by the appearance of the red markings in the spring of the year, Tinbergen concludes that there must be an *innate releasing mechanism* that responds to sign stimuli and is responsible for the instinctive complex of behavior.

As Tinbergen (1952) demonstrates, the stickleback's mating behavior occurs in a very definite and unalterable sequence in which the completion of one phase is necessary to provide the sign stimuli for eliciting the next phase. The stickleback does not begin to build his nest until he has defended the territory for a while. As the first step in nest building, the stickleback digs a small hole. If someone fills up the hole, the stickleback will dig again. Only after many failures will he proceed to build the superstructure without a pit or depression under it. The next phase (courting) normally will not occur until the nest-building phase is completed. If a female enters the territory before the nest is complete, she will be driven away or at best greeted with a few abortive zigzags, which are the beginnings of the courting behavior.

The clear sequence of "bits" of behavior is best seen in the actual mating. When all is ready, the appearance of a female with an egg-swollen belly elicits in the male a characteristic zigzag dance. The dance elicits courting behavior on the part of the female, which in turn causes him to lead her to the nest. He indicates the entrance to the nest and she enters. The male quivers as he nudges the female near her tail. This induces her to spawn. The presence of eggs induces the male to fertilize them. According to Tinbergen, each step in this sequence can be shown to depend upon a limited set of sign stimuli, very much as the fighting behavior was shown to depend on a red belly. For example, once the female has entered the nest, she can be induced to spawn by stimulation with a glass rod even though she has seen the male who led her there removed from the tank.

The stickleback's behavior is clearly hierarchical—as Tinbergen (1951) indicated. The reproductive instinct, the largest unit, is revealed in the sequence of fighting, nest building, mating, and the raising of the brood. Each of these segments is composed of smaller units in the hierarchy. For example, the male's mating behavior consists of a zigzag dance, leading the female to the nest, showing her the entrance, quivering to induce her to spawn, and fertilizing the eggs.

This sort of instinctive behavior is complex, inflexible, automatic, and mechanical. It shows very little variability and no learning. When interfered with, instinct appears blind and stupid—as in the case of the stickleback who attacked the mail truck.

IMPRINTING

A second class of behavior in which variability and learning are minimal is *imprinting*. The term applies to the attachment of a complex behavior pattern to a stimulus which happens to be present at the right moment. This is in contrast to the link between instinctive behavior and highly specific sign stimuli. An example of imprinting is the tendency of newborn animals or newly hatched fowl to follow whatever object is seen first. Konrad Lorenz (1935), the European naturalist, noted that if incubator-hatched ducklings saw only him when they were first removed from the incubator, they tended to follow him around very much as normal ducklings tend to follow their mothers.

Imprinting manifests nearly all of the characteristics of instinctive behavior. However, since imprinting depends to some extent upon the experience of the organism, learning is involved—although of a special limited kind. The limitations of the adaptiveness of imprinting can be seen in the way cichlid fish (Cichlidae) identify their young. Baerends and Baerends (1950) report that some of these perch-like fish "learn" to confine their parental behavior to the young of their own species from their experience the first time they raise a brood. This "learning" was demonstrated by the following experimental procedures: Using a pair of young fish about to hatch their first brood, the experimenters exchanged the eggs for those of another species. The parents accepted the brood that hatched and raised them as their own. In subsequent seasons, however, they killed their own young as soon as they hatched, and would never again raise young of their own species, although they would raise a brood of the species they had first raised.

Following Lorenz's report (1935) of imprinting in birds, a great many studies were carried out to test for imprinting in species ranging from insects to mammals. The results were generally positive, indicating that the mechanism of imprinting is widespread and general.

Some of the most interesting, extensive, and experimentally precise studies have been reported by Hess (1958, 1959, 1964). In most of his experiments, he observed ducklings and young chickens in the laboratory or under carefully controlled conditions on an experimental farm. The procedures used in some of the early laboratory experiments (Hess, 1959) illustrate the general nature of the experimental methods used. Eggs of relatively wild mallard ducks were incubator-hatched. The newly hatched birds were placed in small cardboard boxes so they could see very little in the dim light. The duckling could be released in the imprinting apparatus by remote control. The apparatus (see Figure 2.2) consisted of a

Figure 2.2

The apparatus used in the study of imprinting. (Adapted from Hess, 1959, by permission of the author and publisher.)

circular runway formed by plexiglas walls; the runway was about 12 inches wide, 12.5 feet in circumference, and about 5 feet in diameter. A mallard duck decoy was suspended about 2 inches above the runway. The decoy contained a loudspeaker and a heating unit and could be moved around the runway. The movements of both the decoy and the duckling were recorded automatically, and the duckling could be returned to its box automatically through a trap door.

For the imprinting process, the duckling would be released in the apparatus about a foot behind the decoy, the sound would be turned on, and the decoy would emit a human rendition of "gock, gock, gock, gock." Shortly afterward, the decoy would begin to move. The duckling would be permitted to remain in the apparatus a given length of time or to make a specific number of turns before being returned to his small box to await testing.

After the imprinting procedure, two models were placed in the apparatus: the decoy model of a male that had been used during the imprinting procedure, and a female model that differed only in coloration. The duckling was released halfway between the models and given a minute in which to make a decisive following response to one of the silent models. When sound was turned on, the male model emitted the same "gock" sound that had been used in imprinting, and the female emitted a recording of the sound of a real female mallard calling her young. Tests were then run in which the ducklings could choose to follow one or the other of the models. Different tests involved various combinations of the two models, which might be silent or calling, or might be stationary or moving. During the tests most ducklings responded to the male model, thus showing imprinting.

One characteristic that distinguishes imprinting from learning is the *critical period*. It is generally thought that the time during which imprinting can occur is limited to a brief period in the life of the organism. Hess carried out the imprinting procedure with groups of ducklings from one to 32 hours after hatching. Figure 2.3 shows that those ducklings imprinted when they were 13 to 16 hours old showed the greatest effectiveness of the procedure.

The dramatic rise and fall of the curve in Figure 2.3 invites speculation. According to Hess (1959), both are attributable to the amount of "following" behavior that occurred at each age level. The amount of following increased with a growing locomotor capacity after hatching, and then decreased with a growing capacity for fear and resultant unwillingness to follow a strange object. To support his hypothesis, Hess kept the length of time the duckling was exposed to the model constant in one experiment but varied the distance that the model traveled during the imprinting process. The results can be seen in Figure 2.4, where the relationship between the imprinting score and the distance traveled is clear. In a second study, in which the exposure time was varied but the distance was held constant, no difference in effectiveness was found. In a study with newly hatched White Rock chicks, the chicks displayed

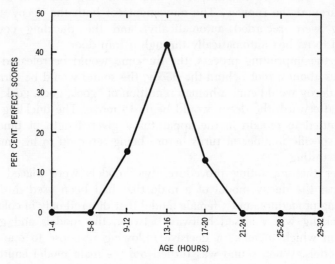

Figure 2.3

If an animal made a positive response to the male decoy on which it had been imprinted in each of the four test conditions, it was given a score of 100 percent, and imprinting was regarded as complete. The figure shows the percent of animals of each age that were completely imprinted according to this criterion. (Adapted from Hess, 1959, by permission of the author and publisher.)

no fear up to 13 to 16 hours after hatching. After this point, the percentage showing fear increased until all animals showed fear at 33 to 36 hours after hatching. Hess's evidence supporting a "critical period" for imprinting is fairly persuasive. Of the large number of variables studied by Hess, several are of special interest or importance. In one set of studies (1964), birds were shocked during the imprinting procedure. Under most circumstances, shock will produce avoidance behavior. But Hess generally obtained more following behavior and stronger imprinting with shock than without. The maximum effect of shock occurred when the birds were 18 hours old. The difference between the disruptive effect of shock in learning and the enhancing effect of shock in imprinting is one of the differences on which Hess bases the conclusion that learning and imprinting are clearly distinguishable.

In another set of studies, chicks were given an opportunity to obtain food by pecking at a green triangle but not at a blue circle for which they showed a preference before reinforcement. When the chicks were rewarded or reinforced for pecking at the green triangle for two hours

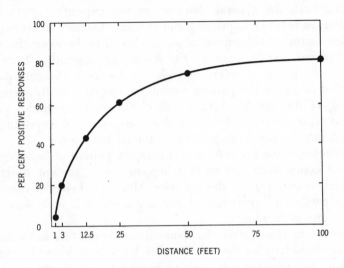

Figure 2.4

Strength of imprinting as a function of the distance traveled by ducklings, with exposure time held constant. (Adapted from Hess, 1959, by permission of the author and publisher.)

on the third day after hatching, something like imprinting, as distinguished from normal learning, occurred. Normally, when such a response is rewarded, or reinforced, and the reinforcement is subsequently removed, the response will gradually disappear—it will undergo "experimental extinction." (When the training took place before or after the third day, the response tended to disappear more or less rapidly when it was no longer rewarded.) But when the training occurred on the third day, the response was highly resistant to extinction and persisted without further reinforcement over a number of days. Hess cites this difference in behavior as further evidence for a difference between imprinting and learning.

Hess has also examined the effects of drugs on imprinting. Some of these tranquilizing drugs either prolonged the period during which imprinting could occur (presumably by reducing the fear response) or prevented imprinting from occurring (presumably by reducing the capacity for effortful muscular response [Hess, 1959]). In studies of the reinforcement of pecking the green triangle, drugs were used which either had not affected normal learning or else had enhanced it. These drugs prevented the imprinting of the pecking response to the green triangle on the third day (Hess, 1964).

These imprinting studies were selected to illustrate several points concerning both the general character of the imprinting process and the differences between imprinting and learning. Lorenz (1935) regarded imprinting as the establishment of an emotional tie between the young and the parent. While many of the studies of imprinting have dealt with the attachment of following behavior to some stimulus pattern, usually that of one of the parents, not all imprinting is of this type. The imprinting of the pecking behavior of chicks on the stimulus pattern associated with reward makes clear that the process of imprinting is a somewhat more general mechanism in animal behavior.

Imprinting is the association of a complex pattern of behavior with a stimulus complex or pattern that happens to be present during the first or early occurrences of the behavior. Thus, it is behavior that varies with the particular experience of the organism and, in a sense, is a primitive form of learning.

However, as Hess (1964) has pointed out, imprinting has a number of special characteristics that set it apart from most learned behavior: (1) Imprinting can occur only during a limited or critical period. (2) Imprinting is prevented by certain drugs, such as tranquilizers. (3) Imprinting is most effective when the training experience is confined to a relatively short space of time and is thus massed rather than spaced (see Hess, 1964). (4) The behavior to be imprinted and the imprinting itself are both accelerated by a noxious stimulus applied during the imprinting process. (5) In imprinting, the *first* experience with a situation is most important. As we shall see subsequently, more complex forms of learned behavior tend to exhibit characteristics quite different from those of imprinting.

EARLY-EXPERIENCE STUDIES

The earliest experiences in the life of an individual organism are sometimes given overriding importance in theories of personality and psychological development. (Examples will be found in McNeil, *The Concept of Human Development,* 1966, and Blum, *Psychodynamics: The Science of Unconscious Mental Forces,* 1966, both in this series.) The designation *early-experience studies* is used to refer to studies demonstrating the *necessity* of certain kinds of early experience for the normal development of an organism. The absence of such early experiences and opportunities for learning appears to restrict the capacity for later learning and thus to prevent normal development.

The most explicit characterization of the differences between early and late learning were developed by Hebb (1949). He hypothesized two kinds of neurophysiological mechanisms underlying the two kinds of learning. The earliest learning, in Hebb's language, consists of the establishment of *cell assemblies*, the most fundamental building blocks of behavior. When a child learns to identify an object, this identification involves a specific neural structure—or cell assembly—which becomes organized during his repeated experiences with the object. In sharp contrast to imprinting, the formation of cell assemblies is assumed to take place slowly and to involve repeated experience. Later learning, according to Hebb, consists largely in the formation of *phase sequences*—as cell assemblies are chained together to produce complex meaningful behavior. Thus cell assemblies might underlie our understanding of individual words, while the chaining of words into meaningful language might represent the formation of phase sequences. In contrast to the slow, early learning and relative stability of cell assemblies, phase sequences are assumed to be learned later and more rapidly and to be easily modified. The concepts *cell assembly* and *phase sequence* are basic to the early-experience studies stimulated by Hebb's work.

This is the line of reasoning that supports early-experience studies: If an animal is deprived of some of the normal childhood (or puppyhood) experiences that normally result in the formation of the requisite cell assemblies, later learning, since it consists of the chaining of cell assemblies into phase sequences, will be distorted or impossible. It is thus clear why the earliest experiences of the organism are considered to be of overriding importance.

In early-experience studies, either animals are deprived of certain normal early experiences or the character of the early experience is rigidly controlled. Efforts are then made to determine the effects of these abnormal early conditions on the later behavior of the animals. One of the most comprehensive of these studies, involving the isolation of Scottie dogs, was carried out in the laboratories at McGill University. Among numerous reports published on these studies are those of Melzack and T. H. Scott (1957) and Thompson and Melzack (1956). J. P. Scott (1962) made a general review of critical periods in behavior development.

The McGill Scotties were isolated after they were weaned at about four weeks of age. They remained isolated in cages until they were about eight months old and were essentially adult. The ten isolated dogs could not see out from their cages although light was admitted from above. The cages had two compartments with a sliding door between to permit provisions of food and water and for cleaning the compartments. Melzack and Scott (1957) compared the behavior of these ten isolated dogs with that of twelve littermates who were raised as pets in homes or had a "normal" or "unrestricted" rearing in the laboratory. After the isolated dogs were released from confinement, they were exceptionally active and playful. According to Thompson and Melzack (1956) the isolated dogs showed a "puppy-like exuberance" that seemed strange in an animal that appeared to be physically adult. Thompson and Melzack also report more formal tests of exploratory behavior. Several normal and several restricted dogs were tested individually in a small room for 30 minutes on each of four days. The normal dogs soon became bored with the monotony of the room and quietly relaxed. The restricted dogs continued to explore for a "considerably longer time." Similar results were obtained in a series of four 10-minute tests in a maze where the amount of activity of the dogs could be easily quantified.

The reactions of the dogs were also observed in the presence of a series of strange objects such as a human skull, a slowly filling balloon, and an open umbrella. The normally-reared Scotties ran away from such objects. The isolated Scotties "became highly agitated, jumped back and forth near the object, whirled around it, stalked it. . . ." Their behavior was "diffuse" or "undifferentiated." When the isolated dogs were tested again a year later, their behavior was somewhat similar to the original avoidance behavior of normal dogs. The normal dogs, on the other hand, now "attacked the objects with playful aggression," rather than showing fear.

In other tests, the isolated dogs showed "marked deficiencies in learning and problem solving" (Hebb, 1958). In one such test (Thompson and Heron, 1954; Thompson and Melzack, 1956) the dogs were trained to find food by running along a wall from one corner of a room to the next. The food was then placed in another corner of the room in full view of the dog, and the pan was banged on the floor. The normal dogs usually ran straight to the new position. The restricted dogs were much less efficient, often running first toward the corner where the food had been previously.

The dogs were also presented with a classic test of animal "intelligence," the detour problem. Food was placed behind a wire screen. To reach the food, an animal had to "detour" around the screen. Normal dogs were reported to solve this problem in one or two trials; the isolated dogs spent much time in front of the food, pawing the screen, trying to push their muzzles through, or otherwise trying vainly to get the food that was behind the wire. The restricted dogs were described as displaying "strikingly unintelligent behavior."

One further study involved a series of 18 maze problems that tested a wide variety of abilities. This study might be considered as a test of animal intelligence. All of the dogs were given preliminary training in maze running through simpler mazes, so that they were proficient in performing in mazes of this type. The restricted animals were markedly inferior in their performance on the 18 more difficult mazes. Thompson and Melzack (1956) report that animals that had been out of the restricted environment for several years were still inferior in performance to the normal dog, indicating that the retardation imposed was more or less permanent.

Probably the most dramatic effect of the isolation of the dogs is revealed in tests for the reaction to or perception of pain. Two studies involved the reaction to an electric shock. In one study, the Scotties were placed in an enclosure that measured 3 feet by 6 feet. They were then pursued by a small, remote-control, toy automobile which delivered a strong electric shock on contact. The restricted dogs did not really learn to avoid the car and received more than four times as many shocks on the average as the normal dogs. Two restricted animals tested two years after release received nine and 23 shocks respectively when the average number of shocks received by normal dogs was six. In the second study involving shock, the enclosure was divided in the middle by a 3-inch barrier. The grid floor could be charged to deliver a strong shock. The dogs were placed individually on the side they preferred. The experimenters then made a rule: After one minute, a second of strong shock would be delivered through the floor of that side. However, if the Scottie jumped the barrier during the minute, it could escape the shock. After an escape, the animal was replaced on the shock side. Ten tests were given each day for three days for a total of 30 trials. No further tests were run if an animal avoided the shock five trials in a row. Ten of the twelve normal dogs reached this criterion, while only two of the nine restricted animals did so. Tests on two restricted dogs two years later seem to indicate that the deficiency persisted over that length of time. The authors attribute the differences in the behavior of the two groups of dogs to differences in pain perception. They report that the normal and restricted dogs did not differ either in the threshold for shock or in their reactions to minimum values of shock. The strong shocks used in the tests were obviously painful to the normal dogs.

The conclusion that rearing in the isolated environment has affected the capacity to perceive pain was tested further by means of two kinds of tests. In one, a lighted match was brought near the animal's nose. Normal dogs either will avoid the flame immediately or will quickly learn to do so. Seven of ten restricted dogs made no attempt to get away from the nose-burning match. They moved their noses into the flame as soon as it was presented. They then jerked their heads or whole bodies away "as though reflexively." But they returned to the flame, hovered excitedly rather than retreating, and three of the animals sniffed at the flame as long as it was presented. A similar test consisted in jabbing the animals with a dissecting needle in the skin at the sides of the hind thighs. After this experience, the restricted dogs spent more time near the experimenter than before and generally behaved as if they were "unaware that they were being stimulated by something in the environment."

The authors conclude that the lack of normal early perceptual experience had influenced, at least in part, the development of certain normal overt responses such as avoidance of noxious stimuli and had prevented the normal development of the capacity to perceive normal pain. They relate an anecdote concerning one of the restricted dogs. There was a low pipe in the laboratory room, and one dog was observed to hit his head on the pipe 30 times within an hour. Normal dogs would not and did not perform in this manner. Such behavior could be attributed to a failure to perceive normal pain, a failure to react to the pain with avoidance, or sheer stupidity in failing to remember the earlier experience. That the restricted dogs failed to perceive pain cannot be established, given the subjective nature of the experience of pain, but the possibility cannot be rejected for the same reason.

Whatever the nature of the restricted dogs' deficiencies in situations one would normally regard as painful, there is no doubt that the early isolation of these Scottie dogs had profoundly affected the character of their later development. Furthermore, although the evidence is not wholly adequate, it suggests that equality with the normal littermates was never achieved. Thus the deprivation of normal stimulation during the development phase produced an animal that was deficient in intelligence, in learning capacity, in the normal tendency to exhaust curiosity, in emotionality, and possibly in the capacity to perceive pain. In the words of Thompson and Melzack (1956), the early restriction has produced animals that "may remain forever immature."

SUMMARY

It is the belief of many students of animal behavior that there are extremely complicated patterns of behavior which may be described as *instinctive* and which do not involve *learning*. Such patterns are presumed to be built into the neurosensory structure of the organism, and to be made ready for activation at an appropriate stage of maturity or physiological condition. Ethologists refer to this readiness as an *innate releasing mechanism* which is activated in the presence of a fixed stimulus pattern, a *sign stimulus*. Instinctive behavior is stereotyped, rigid, and is subject to little or no modification through experience.

Imprinting involves the association of a complex pattern of behavior with whatever stimulus pattern is present the first time the behavior pattern appears in the development of the organism. The complex behavior patterns which can be imprinted include following, brood-raising, and pecking at a given stimulus for food. Usually, imprinting can occur only during a *critical period*. This and many other characteristics distinguish imprinting from ordinary learning.

Finally, there seems little doubt that the *early experience* of the individual organism is especially important in its development. Deprivation of normal stimulation during the early phases of growth produces an immature organism whose capacity to learn seems permanently distorted and reduced.

The simplest forms of true learning are *conditioning* and *instrumental learning*. They are quite general—in contrast to imprinting, they do not appear to be limited to particular organisms, stimuli, or responses. Because conditioning and instrumental learning are so simple and general, theorists have held them to be models that reveal the basic nature of all learning. However, their relative merit as paradigms has been and continues to be a controversial issue.

CONDITIONING AND INSTRUMENTAL LEARNING AS PARADIGMS

CLASSICAL CONDITIONING

Conditioning is a form of learning in which the capacity to elicit a response is transferred from one stimulus to another. The example of Pavlov's salivating dog is often cited because it was one of the first formal conditioning experiments. Pavlov (1927) taught one of his laboratory animals to salivate at the sound of a beating metronome by injecting meat powder into the dog's mouth after each of a number of presentations of the sound. Pavlov's conditioning procedures are termed "classical" because of their historic significance in psychology. Perhaps one reason for the prominence of this particular example of conditioning is that most of us find ourselves similarly conditioned to a variety of sights and sounds—our mouths water at the sight, smell, or even thought of a favored food.

The terms that describe conditioning can be illustrated by Pavlov's experiment. The meat powder that produced salivation without training was an *unconditioned* stimulus (*US*) producing an *unconditioned* response (*UR*). After the conditioning procedure, the metronome sound that produced salivation was a *conditioned* stimulus (*CS*) producing a *conditioned* response (*CR*). (Before conditioning, the metronome sound did not produce the relevant response and was therefore a *neutral* stimulus.) These simple relationships are diagramed in Figure 3.1.

In conditioning, the *CR* sometimes appears to be identical with the *UR*, possibly differing only in amount. However, in most circumstances,

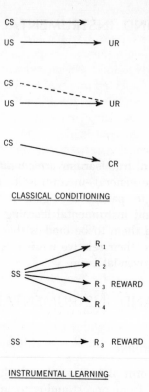

CLASSICAL CONDITIONING

INSTRUMENTAL LEARNING

Figure 3.1

Diagrams of the classical-conditioning and instru-mental-learning paradigms which give rise to sub-stitution and reinforcement models for learning. In the classical conditioning diagram, CS stands for conditioned stimulus; US, unconditioned stimulus; UR, unconditioned response; CR, conditioned re-sponse. In the instrument learning diagram, SS stands for stimulus situation; R for available response.

the two responses are clearly different. Kimble (1961, pp. 52–59) says that the two most commonly held views of the relation between the *UR* and *CR* is that the *CR* is either a fractional component of the *UR* or that it is a preparatory response in anticipation of the *US*.

It is clear that classical conditioning involves substantially more variability of behavior than does instinct or imprinting, both of which are characterized by rigidity, inflexibility, and lack of major variation. Conditioning is generally regarded as the simplest form of true learning.

INSTRUMENTAL LEARNING

The paradigm of instrumental learning is also diagramed in Figure 3.1. It is the essence of instrumental learning that a response is instrumental in the achievement of a goal. Suppose a hungry organism is offered a choice of four responses which are in all respects (save one) equally attractive. The four responses are performed and one of the four (in the diagram, R_3) leads to food. On subsequent occasions, the response that leads to food will be selected and will tend to be dominant whenever the organism is hungry and is in the same "stimulus situation" (SS). This form of learning is called *instrumental learning* because one of the responses is instrumental in goal achievement; it is also called *selective learning* because the rewarded response comes, through learning, to be selected at the expense of the responses which do not lead to the reward.

Instrumental learning involves more variability of behavior and a wider range of responses than classical conditioning does. When faced with a number of equally attractive alternatives, an organism tends to *alternate* between responses. (Thus, in the situation diagramed in Figure 3.1, if the four alternatives are equally likely at the outset, they would each have a probability of occurrence of .25. If the organism chooses R_1 on the first trial, the probability that R_1 will occur on the second trial is considerably reduced, and the probabilities of the other responses occurring on the second trial is raised accordingly. Such "alternation phenomena" occur with high reliability in most instrumental-learning situations.) This tendency to vary responses rather than to repeat them produces more rapid exploration of the environment than would occur by chance.

OTHER PROCEDURES

Several other procedures are frequently employed, although none of them has gained the theoretical importance of classical conditioning and instrumental learning of the response-selection type.

"Avoidance conditioning" is similar to classical conditioning except that performance of the response in avoidance conditioning prevents the occurrence of the US. For example, if a CS tone is followed, inescapably, by the presentation of a shock to the foot of a dog, classical conditioning will occur. In avoidance-conditioning procedure, the apparatus is arranged so that the raising of the foot prevents the shock. Conditioning under classical and avoidance procedures may proceed quite differently, and there is considerable debate concerning the relationship of the two procedures.

"Escape learning" usually involves the application of a noxious US alone in a situation in which the performance of the response leads to escape. In avoidance conditioning, the interval between the CS and the US is usually long enough to permit the response to occur before the US would be applied. If that interval is reduced to the point at which the CS and US appear simultaneously, avoidance is impossible because there is no warning signal, and avoidance conditioning becomes identical with escape learning.

"Temporal conditioning" is another procedure in which a manipulated CS is omitted. The US, such as meat powder, is injected into the dog's mouth without warning, but on a regular temporal schedule. Under these conditions, salivation will tend to occur in a temporal rhythm, in the absence of the US.

Temporal conditioning has been combined with instrumental learning by arranging a situation in which an instrumental response can prevent the occurrence of a noxious US. Thus a rat may be shocked at regular intervals, such as once a minute, unless he presses a bar within the interval. The apparatus may be arranged so that pressing the bar postpones the next shock for some fixed interval, perhaps a minute.

There are numerous other procedural variations, many of which are discussed by Kimble (1961, Chapter 3).

THE GENERALITY OF CONDITIONING AND INSTRUMENTAL LEARNING

It is widely believed that any physical energy change that an organism can respond to in any observable fashion can serve as a CS. There appears to be no evidence contrary to this generalization.

There also seems to be very little limitation on the character of responses that can be conditioned or used as instrumental responses. A great many skeletal movements have been used as UR. Conditioning has been successful with involuntary skeletal responses such as the knee jerk in response to a tap on the patellar tendon. Many types of autonomic responses, such as the galvanic skin response and vasomotor reactions, have been successfully conditioned. Some difficulty is occasionally encountered in the conditioning of simple reflexes such as the patellar reflex and the pupillary reflex (Kimble, 1961). In the period of the past 45 years, some controversy has existed concerning the conditionability of the pupillary reflex to light and to electric shock. Kimble (1961) lists citations of eleven successful and nine unsuccessful attempts, and suggests that success seems more probable when shock is used as the US. Physiological responses such as gastric secretions in response to food, nausea and vomiting induced by morphine, and immunity reactions induced by injections of toxins and antigens have been conditioned. Furthermore, conditioning has been carried out successfully when the CS was direct stimulation of the brain, thus bypassing normal receptor organs, and in which the UR was the blocking of the "alpha rhythm" in the cortex, thus bypassing any normal effector activity. (The alpha rhythm is a characteristic frequency of the electroencephalogram.)

Age appears to be a factor in the ease of conditioning, although there appears to be no age (for which there are suitable CSs and USs) at which conditioning cannot occur. Conditioning has been reported in chick embryos in the fifteenth day of incubation (Hunt, 1949) and in the human fetus in the seventh and ninth months of pregnancy (Spelt, 1948). The sucking reaction of newborn infants has been conditioned to the sound of a buzzer by Marquis (1931). A reduced potentiality for conditioning in older people has been reported by Braun and Geiselhart (1959).

While there is little question concerning the conditionability of higher organisms, controversy does occur in the interpretation of results of experiments demonstrating the classical conditioning of very simple, primitive, invertebrate organisms. Thompson and McConnell (1955) report the classical conditioning of planaria, a simple flatworm. Subsequent investigators have reported mixed success, but there is little doubt that classical conditioning extends well into the invertebrate world (Jacobson, 1963; McConnell, 1966).

CONDITIONING AND "TRUE ASSOCIATION"

Conditioning is presumed to involve the establishment of an *association* between the CS and either the US or the UR. To make certain that such an association has been truly established, it is necessary to distinguish other forms of effects that can occur when the CS is followed by the US. Although it has not often been tested or reported, the occurrence of the CS immediately before the US can influence the character and intensity of the response to the US. The effect can be either an enhancing effect as one would expect if the CS produces an increase in the alertness of the subject, or an inhibiting effect if the CS produces an inappropriate diversion of attention. Such *interaction effects* can occur on the very first presentation.

Another form of change in the response that can occur during conditioning is *adaptation* to the stimuli involved, chiefly to the US. This effect can be demonstrated by presenting the US alone a number of times. Suppose a dog is placed in the stock and harness of the typical conditioning experiment and is shocked on the left forepaw a number of times. The initial reaction may be a violent and generalized threshing about. As the animal is shocked repeatedly, he will gradually become less excited; many responses of a gross bodily character—that serve no function in escaping the shock—will disappear, and the response of lifting the foot will tend to become more precise and deliberate. None of these changes in the response to the shock is generally regarded as associational.

Two other effects noted in classical conditioning that are sometimes regarded as nonassociational are *sensitization* and *pseudoconditioning*.

The augmentation of the response to the CS through the conditioning procedure is called sensitization. On the other hand, presentation of the US can produce a general sensitization of the organism to any stimulus with the result that a response that looks somewhat like the CR can occur on the first presentation of the CS. When such an effect occurs during the course of conditioning, it is referred to as pseudoconditioning.

There are generally two ways of discriminating between pseudo-conditioned responses and true conditioning. In most conditioning experiments, the time interval between the CS and US is sufficiently long (e.g., .5 second) that the CR, when it appears, tends to have a substantial latency—to occur at first only slightly in anticipation of the US. A pseudo-conditioned response, presumably arising from sensitization during conditioning, tends to follow a CS almost immediately. It is frequently possible to separate the responses into two distinct categories on the basis of the latency and to show that pseudoconditioned responses tend to decline in number during training while true conditioned responses, with their longer latencies, are increasing in number. The second way of distinguishing between pseudoconditioned responses and true conditioned responses is by means of appropriate control groups in the design of the conditioned experiment. For example, if one group has 50 paired presentations of the CS and US, a control group might have a random mixture of 50 presentations of the CS and 50 presentations of the US. Any responses occurring to the CS in the control group could be attributed to pseudoconditioning, and the number and course of such responses could be compared with the number and course of responses by the experimental group.

However, not everyone agrees that pseudoconditioning is truly *pseudo* and nonassociational. The CS and US in an experimental situation tend to have much in common that is not shared by other stimuli. Both usually occur in a sound-resistant room with the organism protected from any source of uncontrolled stimulation. Thus both appear and disappear in the same surroundings with sharp onset, sharp offset, and controlled duration. When a response that appears similar to a CR occurs in response to the CS without prior pairing with the US, that response could result from a true association based upon the common character-istics of the two stimuli. This interpretation would explain why the associated response would have a short latency—would occur almost immediately—because the association between sudden onset, for example, and a shock is one of nearly absolute contiguity.

Another phenomenon, conditioned suppression of the UR, has also been noted occasionally. After a number of pairings of the CS and US, the UR may be observed to be diminished in both amplitude and duration. The interjection of a trial in which the CS is omitted may then result in a restoration of the original vigor of the UR. This phenomenon is clearly associational, since it is a product of paired presentation, and has been attributed to Pavlovian inhibition of delay by Kimble and Ost (1961). Inhibition of delay refers to response inhibition in the early part of a long *CS-US* interval.

IS LEARNING A UNITARY PROCESS?

If learning is a single unitary process that can be measured in a number of different ways, various measures of learning should be highly correlated. There are a number of experimental studies in which different measures of learning were obtained in the same situation. A sample of correlations between these learning measures is contained in Table 3.1. In general, such correlations tend to be low. The highest correlations

Table 3.1

Correlations between measures of learning

Authors	CAMPBELL HILGARD (1936)	CAMPBELL (1938)	KELLOGG WALKER (1938)	BROGDEN (1949)
Response	EYE BLINK	KNEE JERK	LEG FLEXION	LEG FLEXION
Organism	MAN	MAN	DOG	DOG
Frequency and Amplitude	.63	.63	.94	
Latency and Amplitude	−.15	−.27	−.22	
Frequency and Latency	−.54	−.27	−.18	
Frequency and Resistance to Extinction		−.60		
Trials to Learn and Trials to Extinguish				.19

tend to occur between the frequency and the amplitude of the response, where the criterion for the occurrence of a response is usually stated in terms of a minimum amplitude, and a substantial correlation is guaranteed. The low correlations could be attributed to errors in measurement and thus low reliabilities of the measures, or one could ask whether different measures might actually be measuring different things.

It has been suggested (1) that amplitude and latency might be most appropriate to autonomic conditioning and (2) that other measures might be more appropriate to the learning of overt movements. This possibility receives some support from the fact that certain variables tend to affect some measures and not others. For example, Hillman, Hunter, and Kimble (1953) report that running speed in a maze is influenced by differences in motivation, while the number of errors is not. Estes (1944) reported that the rate of responding in a lever-pressing task is reduced by punishment, while the number of responses is not. Kimble (1961) has discussed this problem extensively—but no simple solution has emerged.

The role of volition in conditioning is also relevant to our discussion. This issue is not easily resolved, although there have been a number of experimental investigations. Typically, the role of volition has been examined in studies of human eye-blink conditioning. Two examples are a study by Hilgard and Humphreys (1938) and one by Gormezano and Moore (1962). In both studies, variation in instructions to the subjects permitted or discouraged voluntary effort. In both cases, substantial conditioning occurred under "involuntary" instructions (such as not to let voluntary effort influence the response), but the various measures of strength of conditioning all showed greater learning after instructions that encouraged voluntary effort (such as a suggestion that the subject blink so as to avoid the puff of air to the cornea).

Two additional factors should be mentioned. The performance of a response is determined in part by the *strength of learning* and in part by *situational factors*. The greater the effect of situational factors in performance, the smaller the expected correlation between different measures of learning, since different measures might be affected differently. It is also true that both amplitude and latency can be, and often are, learned to some specific value. In avoidance conditioning, the animal learns to respond fast enough to avoid the shock, and in lever-pressing situations, the animal learns to press just hard enough to activate the mechanism. Such criteria, when operating in a situation, would reduce the correlations between either amplitude or latency and any other measure of learning.

Whether learning is a unitary process remains an open question. However, a variety of reactions to the problem have been adopted by psychologists working in the field. Skinner (1938, 1953, 1961) has selected the number of responses and the rate of responding as measures of learning and has chosen to ignore other indices. Tolman (1932) chose to deal only with the percentage of choices distributed among alternatives. Hull (1943, 1952) attempted to develop a complex theoretical formulation that made amplitude, latency, probability of response, and trials to extinction products of a single theoretical variable which he called "excitatory potential." Low correlations were accounted for by introducing a threshold for response and a concept of variability that affected each measure independently.

For the purposes of this book, the question of the unitary character of learning must remain unresolved.

SOME ISSUES OF LEARNING THEORY

CONTIGUITY AND REINFORCEMENT AS PRINCIPLES OF LEARNING

Let us pose a question that is fundamental to learning theory. Is *contiguity* of stimulus and response a sufficient condition for learning, or does learning require *reinforcement?*

We have seen that the temporal contiguity of a CS and a US is important in conditioning. Some theorists rely on conditioning as a model of learning and therefore stress a primary role for contiguity in all learning.

However, an additional principle seems needed to explain selective (instrumental) learning. In the case diagramed in Figure 3.1, the contiguity of the stimulus situation (SS) with each of the four available responses may have been the same. Yet, in the course of the experiment, one response came to be performed in preference to the other three. It is obvious that the food reward distinguished the response that was selected. This reward appears to have *reinforced* the response—to have strengthened the association of the stimulus situation with the response.

There are three main approaches to the problem of contiguity versus reinforcement. (1) One can choose the principle of contiguity as the simplest and most parsimonious way to explain learning. Having made this choice, one must somehow explain selective learning without reference to the principle of reinforcement. This approach is sufficiently attractive that a number of learning theorists have chosen to construct theories which eliminate reinforcement as a necessary condition of learning or which assign it a minor and limited role. (2) One can be a two-factor theorist and assert that, for some kinds of learning, both contiguity and reinforcement are necessary. (3) One can take the position that the principle of reinforcement underlies all learning. Having taken this position, one must show the role of reinforcement in classical conditioning.

It is relatively easy to account for the phenomena of classical conditioning with the principle of reinforcement. In nearly every classical-conditioning situation, some incentive substance, such as meat powder, is present—or there is an aversive stimulus such as shock, the reduction of which could serve a reinforcing role. Since reinforcement always seems to be present in learning, the question of whether or not it is required for learning would seem to be moot.

COGNITIVE AND S-R THEORIES

Another fundamental issue in learning theory is the relative merit of cognitive and stimulus-response theories. A strict S-R theory would limit experimenters to explicit and measurable stimuli and responses (such as grams of meat powder and drops of salivation). A cognitive theory, on the other hand, might speak freely of variables like "expectancy." In the field of learning, all theories have tended to deal with objective-stimulus characteristics and measurable-response properties, but their treatment of variables that intervene between stimulus and response has varied.

According to what might be called *strict behaviorism*, all learning and perhaps all behavior should be described in terms of *overt* stimuli and responses. (The appeal of conditioning as the basis for all learning stems largely from the fact that all its terms are overt, directly measurable, and therefore wholly objective.) Although there is a certain amount of appeal in such an "atheoretical," radical empiricism, almost insurmountable difficulties arise in attempting to apply it. If one follows this approach (sometimes called the "empty organism" approach), one cannot make a distinction between learning and performance—a distinction most theorists find necessary. A simple illustration can be drawn from the example of salivary conditioning in Pavlov's laboratory. The occurrence of the *CR* after conditioning depended on three conditions. Salivation occurred (1) to the sound of the metronome, (2) in the experimental room, (3) when the dog was hungry. The sound of the metronome in the living quarters did not produce salivation even when the dog was hungry. If the dog was not hungry, he did not salivate to the sound of the metronome in the experimental room. In these two situations, it is clear that even though the salivary response had been learned, it was not performed. Thus, the evidence suggests that nonperformance cannot be interpreted to mean that no learning has occurred, although strict behaviorism would apparently require this interpretation.

The major difference between what we shall call *theoretical behaviorism* and a *cognitive* approach is the character of the intervening variables they employ. Theories that adhere to the behavioristic tradition—and use concepts derived from empirical stimulus-and-response research—are frequently referred to as S-R theories. Cognitive theories, on the other hand, tend to use intervening variables that have a cognitive connotation.

Figure 3.2 represents the character of the three positions following the conventions of Walker, *Psychology as a Natural and Social Science* (1967). Strict behaviorism is shown with no intervening variables. (The closest approximation to a strict behaviorism is the theory of Guthrie [1952].) The S-R theory is represented in the diagram by the habit

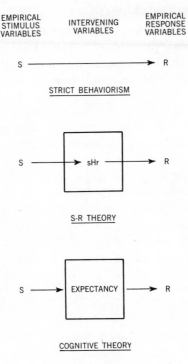

Figure 3.2

Diagrams contrasting the theoretical positions of strict behaviorism, S-R theory, and cognitive theory.

construct of Hull (1943, 1952). The *H*, which stands for "habit," is bracketed by *s* and *r* to indicate that the bond is conceived to be between some internal representation of the stimulus and the response. The equivalent representation of the results of experience in a cognitive theory, such as that of Tolman (1932), is "expectancy."

The issue of whether an S-R theory or a cognitive theory is better cannot really be resolved here, since the difference is largely a difference in experimental strategy. However, there are very practical differences between the two approaches. Adoption of an S-R theory implies a belief that changes in the value of intervening variables will be explained from the findings of strictly controlled conditioning or instrumental-learning experiments. Adoption of a cognitive theory implies that changes occurring with experience may follow principles derived from cognitive research—and may or may not follow strictly from conditioning and instrumental-learning models.

Though the differences between S-R theories and cognitive theories are complex and sometimes subtle, they have generated a great many research studies aimed at establishing one or the other as the better theoretical and research strategy. The question of whether reinforcement or contiguity is the basic principle of learning has been equally powerful in stimulating research. The experiments discussed in the next chapter pertain largely to these two theoretical issues.

The conditioning and instrumental-learning paradigms, as they are diagramed in Figure 3.1, are the predominant models that theorists have used to explain the association and selection of responses. While it is possible to treat the two paradigms separately, there is sufficient similarity of variables and problems relevant to the two to make it possible to organize the research on the learning process in terms of problems rather than in terms of paradigms.

This chapter will treat six basic problems. The most basic problems concern (1) acquisition, (2) transfer, and (3) elimination of learned response; a section will be devoted to each of the three. The next three sections will review research on (4) the nature of reinforcement, (5) explorations of the necessary conditions for learning, and (6) the problem of learning to learn.

ACQUISITION OF RESPONSES

While the response to be learned in both conditioning and instrumental learning is in the repertory of the organism before the learning process begins, the CS *acquires* the capacity to elicit the CR, and the organism *acquires* the tendency to choose one among a number of available alternative responses. A number of basic issues in learning are associated with the acquisition phase of learning.

THE EASE OF CONDITIONING AND INSTRUMENTAL LEARNING

An important issue in both conditioning and instrumental learning is the relative ease with which a given response may be conditioned or learned. It is generally true, in agreement with Pavlov's advice (1927), that any full, vigorous UR may be conditioned.

Conditioning is usually rapid when a sudden, strong, fright-producing stimulus is used. Sometimes, a single pairing of CS and US is sufficient in such a case. Conditioning tends to occur more slowly, if at all, when spinal preparations are used and in certain simple reflexes such as the abdominal, patellar, plantar, and pupillary reflexes. Kimble (1961, pp. 50–52) cites a great many studies demonstrating the controversy over how amenable these responses are to conditioned association.

Since interest is generally in the learning process itself and in the factors which influence the course of learning, experimenters tend to study conditioning that involves responses that are learned neither so rapidly that observation of effects is difficult nor so slowly that the patience of both experimental organism and experimenter is tried.

Instrumental learning problems may be made easy or difficult at will, requiring a single trial or hundreds of trials for successful learning. No one has, as yet, developed a quantitatively meaningful scale of problem difficulty, although many problems would be aided by the development of such a dimension.

THE AMOUNT OF TRAINING

The amount of training in conditioning is usually manipulated in terms of the number of times the CS and the US are paired, while instrumental learning is usually manipulated in terms of the number of trials on which the organism has an opportunity to make the correct response and to be reinforced.

NUMBER OF CS-US PAIRINGS

The tendency of the conditioned response to occur in the presence of the CS alone develops gradually in most conditioning experiments. A number of CS-US pairings is usually necessary. A curve showing the gradual acquisition of the galvanic skin response (GSR) as a function of the amount of training is shown in Figure 4.1. In this study by Hovland (1937c), a tone was used as CS. The US was a mild electric shock to the wrist of the human subjects. The response to the electric shock was a drop in skin resistance. Hovland divided 128 subjects into four groups of 32 subjects each. In one group, the CS and US were paired eight times before the CS was presented alone to test for the strength of conditioning. (The amplitude of the GSR to the CS in the absence of the US was then taken as the measure of the strength of conditioning after eight trials.) A second group had 16 conditioning trials, a third had 24, and a fourth had 48 trials before the CS was presented alone. Figure 4.1 indicates that, with increased training, the magnitude of the CR increased, and, by inference, the strength of the connection between the CS and CR was increased.

The large number of subjects in Hovland's study, combined with Hovland's exceedingly careful experimental control, yields a much smoother curve than is usually obtained. The curve is of the negatively accelerated exponential type. A negatively accelerated exponential curve

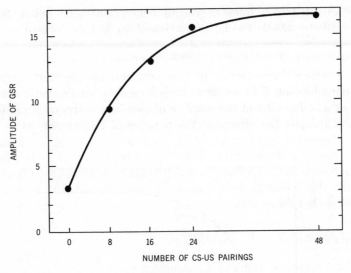

Figure 4.1

Acquisition of a conditioned galvanic skin response. The CS was a sound and the US a mild shock to the wrist of human subjects. (The data are from Hovland, 1937c. Copyright 1937 by the American Psychological Association; reproduced by permission. The drawing is adapted from Figure 21 of Principles of Behavior *by C. L. Hull. Copyright 1943 by D. Appleton Century Co. Reprinted by permission of Appleton-Century-Crofts.)*

is one which gains a constant fraction of the distance remaining to its asymptote on each trial. The negatively accelerated exponential curve is the one that is obtained most frequently in studies of learning, but other curve shapes can also occur. One is an S-shaped curve. In some conditioning procedures, no conditioned response may be detected over a number of trials. This period may then be followed by a rising curve that is positively accelerated, one that gains more on each trial than it did on the previous trial. Such curves then tend to become linear and then negatively accelerated, forming a crude S shape. It will be noted that the latter portion of an S-shaped curve is identical in form with the negatively accelerated curve shown in Figure 4.1. A convincing kind of explanation of the two kinds of curve has been offered by Spence (1956). He suggests the S-shaped curve represents the complete course of conditioning and that negative exponential curves are obtained when the conditioning procedure is applied in situations in which some previous learning is effective. Thus the prevalence of the negative exponential curve arises from the fact that conditioning studies usually involve *CS-US* associations in which some degree of connection exists before training begins; they represent the latter portion of an S-shaped curve.

NUMBER OF TRIALS IN INSTRUMENTAL LEARNING

A learning curve similar to that obtained by Hovland appears in instrumental learning. Learning (which is here equated to habit strength) increases as a function of the number of times the response is reinforced. Figure 4.2 shows the effects of the number of reinforcements on habit

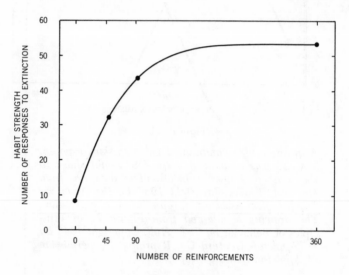

Figure 4.2

Effect of number of reinforcements on habit-strength measures in terms of number of trials to extinction. (Adapted from Harris and Nygaard, 1961. Copyright 1961 by Southern Universities Press; adapted by permission of the authors and publisher.)

strength. Harris and Nygaard (1961) studied rats pressing a lever. One group of rats was given 45 reinforcements in one day; another group 90 reinforcements in two days; another 360 reinforcements in eight days. When reinforcement was removed, the number of responses to extinction (disappearance of the response after reinforcement has been removed) was recorded. The point on the curve for no reinforcements was obtained by fitting a curve to the other three points and determining the zero value by extrapolation. This curve is almost indistinguishable from the conditioning curve obtained by Hovland in classical conditioning and shown in Figure 4.1.

OVERLEARNING

Another curve form that occurs occasionally in conditioning studies is one that rises and falls under continued pairing of the CS and US. An example may be seen in Figure 4.3. In this experiment three rats

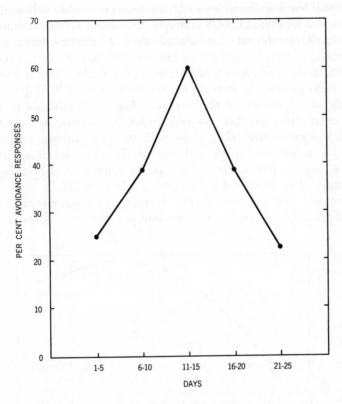

Figure 4.3

Percent avoidance responses of three rats trained under three different CS-US intervals. The rise and fall of the learning curve occurred under continued pairing of the CS and US. (The study is by Walker and Earl as reported in Walker, 1964. Copyright 1964 by the Nebraska University Press. Curve adapted by permission of the author and publisher.)

were trained to raise their heads to a 60 degree angle from the horizontal, a head position which avoided a dazzling light. The CS was a tone, and the CS-US intervals were three, five, and 10 seconds, with each animal conditioned at a different CS-US interval. Each animal had five trials a day for 25 days with a mean intertrial interval of about 40 seconds. The tendency to respond by lifting the head first increased and then decreased over the 25 day period. The increase and decrease in *performance* under continuation of the conditions that produced the *learning* was of interest to Pavlov (1927), although he did not investigate it extensively. Hilgard (1933) published a figure showing an S-shaped curve followed by a decline under continued *CS-US* pairing in human eyelid conditioning, and Hovland (1939) referred to it as attributable to the "inhibition of reinforcement." No simple explanation has been offered. Since the response to the *US* tends to adapt or to decrease in magnitude within a few trials, it is common practice to increase the intensity of the *US* within the first few trials of acquisition of the response. The usual effect is to restore the response. However, there are times when an increase in the intensity of the *US* is ineffective. This, along with the phenomenon indicated in Figure 4.3, seems to require a distinction between learning and performance, since performance declines under conditions of learning. This distinction will be discussed more fully in a later section.

Increasing the number of reinforcements in instrumental learning does not always lead simply to asymptotic performance. There are times

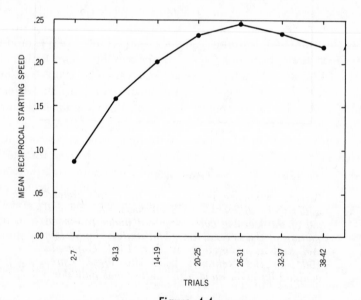

Figure 4.4

A curve that rises and falls under continued reinforcement. Starting speed of animals given one trial a day in a runway for 42 days with 32 grams of wet mash as a reward. (The data are from Ashida, 1963, as they appeared in Walker, 1964. Copyright 1964 by the Nebraska University Press. Curve adapted by permission of the author and publisher.)

when performance tends to decrease as a result of overlearning. An example may be seen in Figure 4.4. In this study by Ashida (1963), a rat's starting speed in a simple runway rose and then began to fall under continued reinforcement. In an earlier study by Kendrick (1958), thirsty animals running for water were reported first to have increased running speed and then to have decreased speed until all animals refused to run at all even though water was still available at the end of the maze. Fuchs (1960) failed to replicate the Kendrick results, but there can be little doubt that there are conditions under which increasing numbers of reinforcements result in decreasing performance. It seems likely that, in these conditions, habit strength either continues to increase with training or becomes asymptotic, and therefore has a fixed value, while the incentive value of the reward undergoes a change.

EXTERNAL INHIBITION

Pavlov (1927) observed that the introduction of a novel stimulus during conditioning will usually produce a decrement in the response. He named the phenomenon *external inhibition*. Whether a novel stimulus will produce a decrement or an increment in the value of the response depends on the character of the response being learned and the character of the response induced by the novel stimulus alone. In a situation involving instrumental learning, Winnick and Hunt (1951) produced response decrements in running speed by presenting a novel stimulus, a four second buzzer, just before the gate was raised to allow the animal access to an elevated runway. When the buzzer was introduced for the first time on the fourth training trial, it took the experimental animals more than 30 seconds to run; the control group—without the novel stimulus—ran in less than 10 seconds. As training proceeded, the amount of decrement produced by the introduction of the buzzer for the first time became progressively less. Thus, on the fourteenth trial, the control group ran the maze in 2.3 seconds, while the experimental group, experiencing the buzzer for the first time just before this trial, required 3.89 seconds. Similar decrements in response have been shown to result from the removal, as opposed to the addition, of a part of the stimulus complex (Fink and Patton, 1953).

A novel stimulus can induce an increase in the measured value of a CR. Kimmel and Greene (1964) conditioned the GSR to a visual stimulus in human subjects, and introduced an auditory stimulus (a 3,000 cps tone) during the presentation of the CS at different stages of training for different groups. Before training, both the CS and the novel tone produced a GSR, and both stimuli presented together produced a larger GSR than either alone. As training proceeded, the GSR to the CS increased and then decreased slightly. Addition of the novel tone for the first time, however, had an increasingly dramatic effect of producing a progressively increasing amplitude of the *GSR*. On the fiftieth trial of training, the *CS* and the novel tone together produced about 10 times the *GSR* response that was produced by the *CS* alone. Thus, the introduction of a novel stimulus during training can produce either a response decrement or response increment, and is probably inappropriately named *external inhibition*.

Note that the addition or subtraction of a stimulus creates a new and *different* situation. When a response—such as a *GSR*—is carried over from one situation to another, it is called a *generalized response*. Stimulus and response generalization will be discussed in the next section of this chapter on the transfer of responses.

INTENSITY VARIABLES

THE DISTINCTION BETWEEN HABIT AND DRIVE

Theorists usually distinguish between habit and drive on the basis of the distinction between learning and performance. Suppose we place a hungry organism in a complex situation in which food is available if the organism solves a problem. At first, the organism is active, but his performance is poor. After a number of trials, he learns to perform the response quickly and without error. Suppose that later we place him in the same situation when he is not hungry. His performance is likely to be again poor, even though we have no doubt that he has learned to solve the problem.

If habit (H) and drive (D) determine performance (P), one possible relationship between these variables is:

$$P = H \times D.$$

Thus, the value of P will be low if either D or H is low, and will be maximal only when both D and H are high (i.e., when the animal has learned to solve the problem and is motivated to do so). The terms "habit" and "drive" are fairly specific to S-R theory (discussed on page 26), but most theories of learning make a similar distinction. Thus, the term "habit" might be exchanged for any number of other terms that represent the role of *historical* variables—those that determine what the organism "knows" about the situation on the basis of previous experience. The term "drive" might be exchanged for other words that refer to the *situational* variables—those that influence performance. These are essentially the ones that can be manipulated between trials or experiences in the situation.

DRIVE LEVEL AND PERFORMANCE

There is general agreement that, if H is held constant, performance will first increase and then decrease as drive is increased. A curve

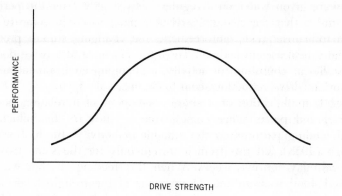

DRIVE STRENGTH

Figure 4.5

*Inverted-U curve showing relationship of perform-
ance as a function of drive strength.*

showing the relationship between performance and drive might look
something like the inverted *U*-shaped function in Figure 4.5. A number
of explanations have been offered for this shape. One possibility is that
as the time without food grows longer and longer, the organism becomes
more and more active until he starts to grow weak. As he approaches
starvation, his performance declines until, if no food becomes available,
he eventually dies. On the other hand, poor performance sometimes
occurs in conditions of high motivation and appreciable habit strength,
even though physical weakness is not a factor. It has been suggested
that the greater the habit strength, the stronger the drive can be without
producing deterioration in performance. This phenomenon is sometimes
referred to as the Yerkes-Dodson Law (1908). Thus the athlete with
little skill does poorly under pressure, while the highly skilled athlete
produces his best performance when the pressure is greatest.

A curve such as that in Figure 4.5 is the kind most generally expected
when performance is simple activity or a specific goal-directed performance. However, there have been studies of the strength of drive in which
such a curve has not been obtained. For example, Hall, Low, and
Hanford (1960) reported no differences in the activity of hungry and
satiated animals in a Dashiell checkerboard maze. One explanation of
such failures has been offered by Sheffield and Campbell (Sheffield and
Campbell, 1954; Campbell and Sheffield, 1953; Campbell, 1960). They
suggest that no difference in activity level will appear in an unchanging
environment. What these experimenters found was that when activity was
measured in the presence of stimulus changes occasioned by the operation of ventilation fans and the switching on of lights, deprived animals
increased their activity more than nondeprived. Furthermore, if deprived

animals were given water on a regular basis shortly after the period of stimulation—so that the changing stimulus patterns could come to serve as a cue for subsequent reinforcement, the changing stimuli produced even greater increases in activity. Thus, the presence of a drive does not seem a sufficient condition for activity; a changing environment and the expectation of drive reduction seem to be necessary factors.

Another modification of a simple statement of a relation between drive level and performance comes from a study of the influence of temporal feeding patterns on the amount of activity. Birch, Burnstein, and Clark (1958) fed rats from a trough only for the same two hour period each day for five weeks. When this feeding rhythm was well established, food was omitted. Depressions of the trough, taken as the measure of activity, were narrowly confined to the period of usual feeding, and declined during the hours when the animals were not normally fed. This study appears to make clear that the relation between the drive strength and activity may frequently be affected by learned temporal rhythms.

CS INTENSITY

Does the strength of the CS influence the strength of association in conditioning? If conditioning proceeds equally well with very weak stimuli and with intense ones, the frequency with which conditioning occurs under everyday circumstances would be very much greater than would be the case if effective conditioning occurred only with very strong stimuli. Unfortunately, the problems involved in experimental demonstrations of the effects of stimulus intensity upon the strength of the association (as opposed to the vigor of the performance of the response) appear nearly insurmountable. The difficulty in demonstrating the effect of CS intensity on the strength of conditioning is best seen in the context of a well-designed study. Grant and Schneider (1949) conditioned the GSR response in human subjects by pairing a tone with a shock to the wrist. Sixteen groups of five subjects were used. Four intensities of CS were used during training and during extinction of the response. Each of the groups was trained with one CS intensity; then extinction was carried out with either the same or a different intensity. The procedure involved 10 trials of adaptation to the sound of the tone alone, 20 paired presentations of the CS and US, and then 10 extinction trials with one of the CS intensities presented alone. The score of each group was the sum of the magnitudes of the GSR's during the extinction trials. The results are shown in Table 4.1. The logic of this design is precise. The means of the rows represent the differences in learning attributable to CS intensity. Since these differences do not show an orderly relationship to CS intensity during conditioning, Grant and Schneider conclude that CS intensity cannot be said to have affected strength of conditioning. The

Table 4.1

Effects of CS *intensity during conditioning and extinction as measured by the magnitude of the* GSR *during extinction (Grant and Schneider, 1949).*

		CS intensity (dB) during extinction				
		76	86	96	106	Means
	106	199.5	77.6	155.8	230.8	165.8
CS intensity (dB)	96	119.8	297.4	258.6	427.4	275.8
during conditioning	86	119.0	155.6	331.4	270.8	219.2
	76	265.1	213.0	180.2	244.2	225.7
Means		175.8	185.9	231.5	293.3	221.6

means of columns represent the effects of the intensity of the CS during extinction, since each mean has an equal representation of each CS intensity during conditioning. Here, the orderly increase in score with increase in CS intensity, along with other evidence from the study, supports the conclusion that the intensity of the CS during extinction does affect the performance of the response.

Grant and Schneider's additional conclusion, that the intensity of the CS does not affect the strength of learning (conditioning), is probably a sound one, yet there are some residual unresolved problems. The conclusion rests on the assumption that the generalization gradient for intensity (tendency to make some response to stimuli differing in intensity from the CS) is a straight line, and that generalization effects are equal in the testing stage. This assumption is reasonable, but not certain, and in this case is supported by the fact that no significant generalization effects are apparent in the data. On the other hand, the data reflect considerable variability. It is conceivable that some effect of CS intensity during conditioning might have been found with an extremely large number of subjects, and positive results might have been found with a greater range of CS intensities.

US INTENSITY

The logic of the design of a conditioning study to show the effect of the intensity of the US on learning, as opposed to performance, is similar to the problem of the intensity of the CS, but the problems of interpretation are more difficult and involved. Spence (1953) has reported a study of the intensity of the US that will serve as an example. He conditioned a group of 80 men, using an increase in the brilliance of an illuminated disc as a CS and a puff of air to the cornea as the US, to produce a reflexive wink. The CS lasted 825 milliseconds, and the US came on 755 milliseconds after the CS and lasted for 50 milliseconds. On the first day, half of the subjects had a weak puff (.25 lbs./sq. in.) as the US, and the other half had a strong puff (5.00 lbs. per sq. in.) as the US. Each group had 30 conditioning trials on the first day. On the second day they had 20 additional paired presentations of the CS and US, but for half of each group, the intensity of the US was changed to the other value. The frequencies of CRs in the four groups during the 20 trials of training during the second day were then reported. The logic

Table 4.2

Effects of US intensity on learning and performance. Mean number of CRs made in first 20 trials of day 2 (Spence, 1953).

		Day 2 US (pounds per square inch)		Means (Learning)
		.25	5.00	
Day 1 US (pounds per square inch)	.25	5.65	8.80	7.23
	5.00	7.45	13.00	10.23
Means (Performance)		6.55	10.90	

is similar to that in the study of CS intensity above. Spence argues the following interpretation: Within each column, the US intensity was different on Day 1 and the same on Day 2. Therefore, the difference in number of CRs, e.g., the difference between 8.80 and 13.00, must be attributed to the difference in US intensity on Day 1. The implication is that the different intensities of US produced different amounts of learning on Day 1. Within each row, the US intensity was the same on Day 1, but different on Day 2. Therefore, the difference in number of CRs, e.g., the difference between 5.65 and 8.80, is a joint product of the effect of different intensities of US on both learning and performance on the second day.

Among the problems which make interpretation of the results difficult are the following. (1) Different US intensities may be regarded as producing qualitatively different responses and not simply the same response differing only in vigor. (2) Different responses may differ in ease of conditioning, and the differences in Table 4.2 might be due to qualitative differences in the responses. (3) There is an implicit assumption that the loss in response strength through intensity generalization is the same when one changes from a weak to a strong stimulus as when one changes from a strong stimulus to a weak one. (4) The performance on the second day of training represents a confounding of the effects of the US intensity on learning and performance within that day. These problems, and others, were discussed by Spence. Many subsequent efforts have been made to demonstrate the differential effects of US intensity on learning and performance. These studies involve the manipulation of many kinds of variables and the use of complicated logic and experimental designs (for example, see Spence and Tandler, 1963). No completely satisfactory resolution to the problem is available.

The duration of the US might be looked on as a variable that influences the intensity of the effects of the US. The duration of the US has also been of special interest to theoretical positions such as those of Mowrer (1960) who attributed different roles to the onset and the offset of the US. Kimble (1961) interprets a number of such studies as showing no effect of duration.

EFFECT OF DRIVE STRENGTH ON LEARNING

Despite its importance, the question of the effect of drive strength on habit strength has proved nearly unsolvable. This problem is similar to that involved in the analysis of the effect of US intensity on strength of association. When drive strength is varied during learning, higher drive produces a higher performance level. To test whether this difference reflects a difference in habit strength, the standard procedure is to reverse the drive levels for half of each group during further training or extinction. The difficulties involved in interpreting such data in terms of the effect of drive strength on learning may be seen in a study by Butter and Campbell (1960): They trained two groups of rats to run in a straight runway. They varied drive strength by giving the animals either 3 or 10 grams of their daily 15 grams of food 30 minutes before testing. Animals given only 3 grams were assumed to be high-drive animals and those given 10 grams were considered to be low-drive animals. They ran two trials a day for five days under the original drive conditions with 2 grams of food reward on each trial. At the end of the first block of five days, the levels of hunger drive were reversed for the two groups. On the eleventh day they were reversed again, and the reversal process continued through five blocks. Thus the drive levels for one group were high-low-high-low-high in successive blocks of trials, and for the other group they were low-high-low-high-low. The results are plotted in Figure 4.6. The most general result is that the group that started at high drive ran faster throughout the 25 days than the group that started at low drive.

The logic of the drive-reversal experiment can now be applied to the results of any successive pair of blocks of trials. Let us add another term

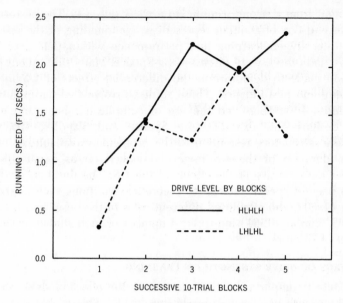

Figure 4.6

*Mean running speed plotted as a function of suc-
cessive reversals of the hunger drive. Each point is a
mean of 10 trials in five days at one drive level.
Each group was reversed in drive level after each
block of 10 trials. (Adapted by Butter and Campbell, 1960. Copyright 1960 by The American Psychological Association and reproduced by permission.)*

to the expression of the determiners of performance, I, for incentive.
The general formula is:

$$P = D \times H \times I.$$

Let us compare the performances of the two groups on the first two
blocks of trials in Figure 4.6 combined. The incentive (I) is equal for
the two groups, because 2 grams of food was given each animal on each
trial through both blocks. Drive (D) should be equal, because each
group was under each drive for one whole block, and the mean of the
performances for the first two blocks should represent each drive strength
equally. If both D and I are equal for the groups, then differences
in performance must be due to differences in habit strength, H. The
performances are different between the two groups when the first and
second blocks are combined; they are also different when any other pair
of successive blocks is combined—the group which had the high drive
first is consistently found to run faster. Is the habit strength higher in
this group, and if it is, why should it be? The only difference between

the two groups is that one started the experiment at a low drive and the other started at a high drive. It would be possible to argue that habit strength, H, should also be equal between the two groups, since they had had equal numbers of trials under each drive strength. Yet performance in the second block is essentially the same, even though the drive strengths differ, and the near identity can presumably be accounted for by assuming different values of H.

One can account for these results only by either challenging the logic of the drive-reversal experiment or questioning the applicability of that logic in this particular instance. The first course is difficult and unlikely to offer a simple resolution in a short treatment. Butter and Campbell (1960) offer an explanation of their results which questions the applicability of the logic and at the same time poses a general problem for all similar research designs on the problem. The logic assumes (1) that if stimuli arising from the drive state itself are a part of the problem, then they differ only in intensity; (2) that the response of running down the runway is in all cases the same in character, but differs only in vigor. Cotton (1953) did a runway experiment in which drive strength was varied, and in which he counted the number of irrelevant or interfering responses that occurred. If he counted only trials during which no interfering responses occurred, running speed did not differ very much with difference in hunger drive. The implication is that the responses that occur under high and low drive are qualitatively different. Butter and Campbell suggest that in the initial block of learning trials in the experiment, the high-drive animals learned to run, while the low-drive animals learned some incompatible, nonrunning responses. Therefore, the responses learned by the two groups were qualitatively different. Thus, in order to investigate the effect of drive strength on learning, it is necessary to vary drive strength during learning—to do so tends to produce qualitative differences in the responses learned. However, even in the face of these difficulties, the most frequent conclusion is that drive strength affects performance but does not affect the habit strength or the amount learned.

AMOUNT OF REWARD

Do differences in the amount of reward influence performance by changing habit strength, drive level, incentive value, or combinations of these elements? The best tests of this question are probably those in which an effort is made to vary the amount of reward without varying the nature of the consumption of the reward. If an animal is given a large amount of food, his consummatory behavior will be different—more prolonged—than if he is given a small amount of food.

A study that attempted to avoid this problem is one reported by Bower, Fowler, and Trapold (1959). They varied the amount of reinforcement by varying the amount of shock reduction an animal received for running a short runway. They ran three groups of animals with 250 volts on the grid of the starting box and runway. Since the voltage level was the same for all three groups, it is presumed that they were equally motivated. Reinforcement was varied by having the goal box charged with 50 volts less, 100 volts less, or 200 volts less than the runway. The animals were kept in the goal box for 20 seconds after they had reached it. In Figure 4.7, it is apparent that the greater the drop in voltage, the faster the animals ran to get to the goal box, even though the intensity

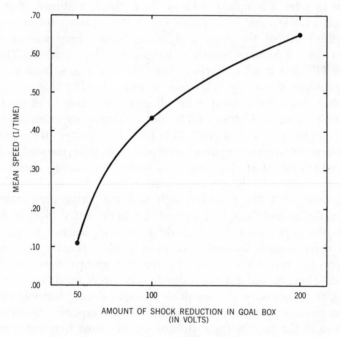

Figure 4.7

Effect of amount of reward—defined as the amount of reduction in shock level in the goal box—on performance. (Drawn from data reported by Bower, Fowler, and Trapold, 1959. Copyright 1959 by The American Psychological Association and reproduced by permission.)

of the shock on the grid was the same for all while they were in the starting box and runway.

A study by Tombaugh and Marx (1965) illustrates another approach to the problem. They varied the amount of reward by presenting all animals with the same amount of liquid to reinforce lever-pressing responses, but varied the concentration of sucrose in the liquid. They trained four groups of eight animals each to press a bar to receive a small dipper full of liquid. Each group had received a different concentration of sucrose. During each of 24 days of the experiment, each animal was reinforced during the first four of eight two-minute periods and was not reinforced during the last four periods. Thus it was possible to measure the number of bar presses per period during reinforcement and during nonreinforcement. Figure 4.8 makes clear that the concentration of sucrose, and thus the amount of reward, did affect performance in both daily phases of the experiment. However, the effects were different in the two phases. Performance during reinforcement appears to increase

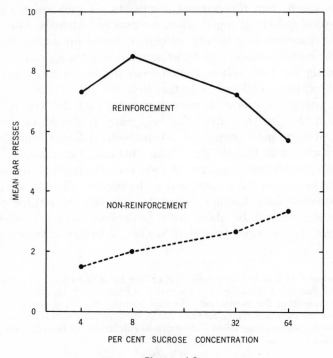

Figure 4.8

Effect of quality of reinforcement on performance during periods of reinforcement and periods of non-reinforcement. (Adapted by permission from Tombaugh and Marx, 1965. Copyright 1965 by The American Psychological Association and reproduced by permission.)

and decrease as the amount of reward increases, while performance during nonreinforcement increases with concentration. Tombaugh and

Marx note that there is evidence that animals tend to spend a greater length of time licking the dipper when the concentration is greater, and there is some possibility that with the stronger solutions, satiation occurs more quickly. This could account for the upper curve in Figure 4.8 in which performance tends to decrease at higher concentrations. The performance during extinction, however, is not affected by any consummatory behavior. It appears to reflect differences attributed to the experiences of the animals during reinforcement.

Different amounts or qualities of reward appear to have their effects upon the incentive value, I, rather than on habit or drive. A further development of the experiment by Bower, Fowler, and Trapold (1959) involved changing the amount of shock reduction in the goal box for subgroups taken from the original groups. In all such subgroups, the running speed quickly changed. Thus, for example, animals shifted from a 200 volt reduction to a 50 volt reduction slowed up within five trials so that their performance was indistinguishable from animals that had been running for a 50 volt reduction from the beginning. Likewise, a group shifted from a 50 volt reduction to a 200 volt reduction speeded up to the performance level of animals running for a 200 volt reduction in shock in the goal box from the beginning. It should be noted in passing that there have been times when results different from those of Bower, Fowler, and Trapold have been obtained. For example, Crespi (1942, 1944) in shifting amounts of food reward obtained an "elation" effect from increasing the amount and a "depression" effect from decreasing the amount. Such findings cannot be ignored, but involve complications which cannot be dealt with here. The Bower, Fowler, and Trapold results are more typical of studies involving incentive shifts.[1]

---

[1] The argument that it is incentive value rather than habit that changes in the Bower, Fowler, and Trapold (1959) experiment is based, at least in part, on the conception of habit as representing the permanent effects of training. By this conception, H may increase but not decrease. Since animals which were running rapidly for a 200 volt reduction in shock slowed up when shifted to a 50 volt reduction, then the only term in the expression

$$P = D \times H \times I$$

that could change to decrease the value of P would be I.

If H can only increase, while I can rise or fall as the incentive is changed, then there are problems with the results of Tombaugh and Marx (1965) in that Figure 4.8 shows an effect of amount of reward on the number of responses under nonreinforcement conditions. With the incentive at a zero value, all performances should be the same. A possible answer is that different amounts of reward produce different amounts of secondary (or learned) reinforcement and that in the Tombaugh and Marx experiment the short extinction period along with the repeated periods of reinforcement and nonreinforcement served to make differential amounts of secondary reinforcement effective during the extinction period.

ACQUIRED DRIVE AND REWARD

The formula that has been used to distinguish the individual effects of drive, habit, and incentive on performance more or less implies that learning consists of a change in the value of H, habit. However, the situation can be considerably complicated by the likelihood that stimuli or objects can themselves acquire the capacity to induce a drive state or can acquire reward value. Thus all three terms—drive, habit, and incentive—may be affected by learning. In fact, it is generally assumed that neutral stimuli, which are designated as "neutral" because they do not appear to have properties of drive, incentive, or reinforcement, can acquire these properties through appropriate conditioning procedures. It is assumed that: a neutral stimulus paired with the *onset* of a strong drive stimulus, such as shock, can acquire drive properties of its own; a neutral stimulus presented in close association with the offset of a drive stimulus such as shock, or with the presentation of a reward such as food or water, can take on incentive and reinforcing properties of its own.

ACQUIRED DRIVE

The classic demonstration of acquired drive is a study reported by May (1948). Rats were trained to jump across a hurdle from one side of a box to the other to escape shock. Once the animals had learned to jump promptly whenever the shock was turned on, the second phase began. In this phase the animals were confined to a small compartment in the center of the apparatus, and given a series of pairings of a buzzer and shock in the classical conditioning paradigm. In the third phase, the small compartment was removed, and the buzzer was sounded alone, without shock. In this phase, about 80 percent of the animals jumped the barrier to escape the buzzer, which was turned off when they jumped. Control animals jumped less promptly and less frequently. Presumably, the buzzer had acquired drive properties to motivate the jumping response. Furthermore, termination of the buzzer may have become an incentive and may have acquired reinforcing properties.

A study by Goldstein (1960) explored the effect of drive strength as represented by shock strength, the number of classical conditioning trials, and the order of the CS and US on acquired drive. In contrast to the demonstration procedure used by May, Goldstein did not give the animals prior training in hurdle jumping. He simply presented a five second CS and delivered shock during the last second of the CS. To test the effect of shock, Goldstein used a two-chamber box; he presented the CS and opened the door between the chambers simultaneously. When an animal jumped the hurdle into the other compartment, the CS was turned off. The test consisted of 15 trials of hurdle jumping in a two hour period; the performance measure was speed of escape. He used three different intensities of shock, and in the test phase the speed of hurdle jumping seemed to increase in an orderly way with intensity of the shock during conditioning. Thus the more intense the shock during conditioning, the stronger the acquired drive. However, Goldstein's results when he manipulated the number of CS-US pairings and the order of CS and US did not follow the pattern to be expected in classical conditioning. He had different groups with either one, three, nine, or 20 CS-US pairings, and speed of hurdle jumping did not increase as the number of conditioning trials increased. Furthermore, he had one group in which the CS followed the most intense shock by 20 seconds, and was thus in a "backward" conditioning pattern; this group jumped the hurdles about as fast as the average performance of the groups with the same number of CS-US pairings in the standard order. Thus, while a neutral stimulus appears to acquire drive properties through classical-conditioning procedures, the acquisition process does not seem to follow all of the laws of classical-conditioning responses.

ACQUIRED REWARD

A demonstration of the power of a secondary reward is that of Ehrenfreund (1949). He set up a simple problem in which rats were required to discriminate between black and white for a food reward. Two groups were run which differed in one respect only. An empty food cup was placed on the incorrect side of a single-choice-point maze for one group and not for the other. Since a food cup was always present when the animal received food, food cups could be expected to take on secondary reward properties. If a cup had secondary reward properties, it could be expected to reinforce the incorrect response to some extent and thus delay the learning of the correct response. In fact, the group with the food cup on the incorrect side did take nearly twice as many trials to learn and made more than twice the number of errors as the other group that did not have the empty food cup on the incorrect side.

This demonstration, alone, does not establish the existence of secondary reward, since it is possible that any additional small object in the incorrect goal box might have made that side more attractive. However, other studies have succeeded in manipulating the secondary reward value of a single stimulus by manipulating variables which could be expected to vary the amount of learning. In a study of bar pressing, Miles (1956) varied the number of times a dim light and click were paired with reward and then extinguished half of his animals with the click and light accompanying the lever press and half without. He found that the greater the number of pairings of the light and sound with food reward, the longer the extinction was delayed. Thus the strength of the secondary reward effect increased in an orderly way with the number of trials. Miles also varied the strength of the hunger drive during extinction and found that the stronger the drive, the longer the animals continued pressing without primary reinforcement. Thus, it is clear that the secondary reinforcement effect is not simply a matter of the presence of any additional stimulus.

Efforts to demonstrate greater secondary reinforcing value for a stimulus paired with a larger reward have frequently been unsuccessful. However, in a study by Butter and Thomas (1958), positive results were obtained. They trained two groups of rats in a Skinner box, giving 0.1 milliliters of solution for each of 48 presses. The reward was an 8 percent sucrose solution for one group and a 24 percent solution for the other. During extinction, for these two groups, the delivery mechanism was allowed to click, but for a control group this source of secondary reinforcement did not occur. The control group gave 3.9 responses in extinction, the 8 percent solution group gave 9.4, and the 24 percent solution group gave 17.6. Thus the click of the mechanism appears to have acquired secondary reinforcing properties and to have been more effective in the group with the higher concentration of sucrose. It is difficult to say for certain that the differences were exclusively attributable to differences in secondary reinforcing properties, for the two experimental groups may have differed during the training phase. However, complete separation of the effects of different qualities of reward on what is learned as opposed to secondary reinforcing effects during extinction is exceedingly difficult logically and experimentally.

Another question of importance is the *specificity* of a secondary reinforcing stimulus to the drive under which it acquired the property. Will a stimulus that acquired secondary reinforcing properties under a thirst drive serve as an incentive and as a reinforcing stimulus under another drive or no drive at all? Estes (1949a, b) trained animals to press a lever for water when thirsty, and then tested them for extinction under either hunger or thirst. He found that the thirsty animals gave the greater number of responses in extinction, but the hungry animals also extinguished slowly in the presence of the click of the mechanism. He concluded that the original drive was not necessary for a secondary reinforcing stimulus to be effective. It was only necessary to have a sufficient drive present to instigate the activity that is to be reinforced.

A very difficult problem in the isolation of the secondary reinforcement effect from other variables in a learning experiment arises from the fact that for an animal to discriminate between one response and another, some cue to the correct response must be provided. This cue, since it is always followed by reward, will become a secondary reinforcer. Thus the same stimulus acquires both a cue function and a reinforcing function. An effort to distinguish between these two functions was made by Dinsmoor (1950). He set up a discrimination problem in a lever-pressing situation. One group of animals was normally in the dark, but the light was turned on to signal the fact that a response would now lead to reward. The first response made after the light came on was reinforced, and the light was turned off when the animal seized a pellet of food and started to eat. The light remained off until the animal had failed to respond for at least 30 seconds. Thus the light became the cue for responding and the darkness became a secondary reinforcing stimulus. A second group had the cues reversed. During extinction, each group was divided, with one half in the dark and the other half in the light. Each response produced a three second change in the light pattern. Thus for half, a response led to the cue for responding, and for the other half, a response led to the secondary reinforcing stimulus. A pair of control groups was extinguished either in continued darkness or continued light, with responses producing no change in the stimulus conditions. Both conditions in which a response during extinction produced a change in the stimulus led to slow extinction compared to the control group, and there was little difference between the two groups. Even though, as will be noted later, stimulus change alone can serve as an incentive in situations of this kind, the failure of the two stimuli to have different effects on extinction represents a failure to show a difference between the cue function and the reinforcing function of stimuli.

In spite of difficulties in separating the secondary reinforcing functions of stimuli from other roles in learning and performance, there can be little doubt that the concept of secondary reward is a meaningful one. Furthermore, in contrast to the results obtained in the case of acquired drive, the acquisition of secondary reward or reinforcement appears to follow the ordinary laws of learning. Miller (1951) has assigned four roles to a stimulus that has acquired secondary reinforcing properties through association with primary reinforcement: (1) It can produce new learning. (2) It can support learned performance and prevent normal extinction. (3) It can serve to bridge a temporal gap between the response and delayed reinforcement. (4) It can have incentive function in that the presence of such a stimulus can produce approach activity.

TIME FACTORS AND TRACE CONCEPTS

Both the rate of learning and the amount learned are dependent upon temporal relationships. In conditioning, the important interval is that between the presentation of the CS and the occurrence of the US. In reinforcement learning, the important interval is between the occurrence of the response and the appearance of the reinforcement. In any learning situation in which training is demarcated in terms of trials, an important interval is the time between trials (the intertrial interval). While the problems are empirical, there is considerable interest in efforts to explain the manner in which two temporally separated events are bound together. One general concept is that of *trace*. If a stimulus occurs at one point in time and can be shown to have an effect on a subsequent event, then it must have left some sort of a trace of itself in the organism. Logically, it is reasonable to talk about stimulus traces, response traces, and memory traces. Furthermore, a distinction is frequently made between an active trace and an inactive one. An active trace is conceived to be a perseveration of neural activity for a period of time after the stimulus is removed. The second kind of trace is thought to involve some structural change in the nervous system that is relatively permanent and can endure for long periods of time.

CS-US INTERVAL

If the CS has sufficient duration, possibly as long as a second, there are two intervals of interest. One is the time from the beginning of the CS to the beginning of the US. The other is the time between the end of the CS and the beginning of the US. The beginning and the end of a CS appear to have different values as cue properties in learning. Kish (1955) ran a pair of studies in which a light either coming on or going off was used as the CS to signal shock. The subject could stop the shock by turning a wheel. Learning was faster at several CS-US intervals when turning the light on was used as the CS.

This difference is reflected in two different conditioning procedures. In *trace conditioning*, the CS is usually brief, and the interval between the onset of the CS and the onset of the US is taken as the CS-US interval. Since no relevant stimulus is presumed to be present during the interval, the effects of the US must then be associated with the trace of the CS. In *delayed conditioning* the CS is continued until the US is presented, and both stimuli are usually terminated together. In this procedure the CS is present when the US is presented, and this bridges the gap between the beginning of the CS and the onset of the US.

There is general agreement that the optimal CS-US interval in classical trace conditioning is approximately .5 second. For example, Reynolds (1945) conditioned a human eyeblink with a click in earphones as the CS and a puff to the cornea as the US. He found a greater number of CRs in 90 training trials when the CS-US interval was 450σ (milliseconds). There were fewer CRs at 250σ and at $1,150\sigma$, and the number of CRs at $2,250\sigma$ did not exceed the number expected when the two stimuli are presented but unpaired. In fact, it is generally believed that no conditioned association takes place in eyelid conditioning when the interval is as long as $2,250\sigma$, or 2.25 seconds.

In other forms of conditioning, longer intervals can lead to association. Kamin (1954) conditioned dogs to jump a hurdle from one compartment of a box to another to avoid a very strong shock. With a number of different measures of learning, he obtained the best performance with a five second CS-US interval in comparison with intervals of 10, 20, and 40 seconds. A sample of his results is plotted in Figure 4.9.

If the CS follows the US, instead of preceding it, the procedure is called *backward conditioning*. In most studies in which the order of the stimuli is reversed, no conditioning occurs. However, there are exceptions. Champion and Jones (1961) made a study of forward, backward, and pseudoconditioning of the human GSR to shock. The CS was a tone of 20σ duration, and the shock lasted 600σ. In the forward-conditioning procedure, the onset of the tone preceded the onset of the shock by 500σ. In the backward procedure, the onset of the shock preceded the onset of the tone by 750σ, leaving an interval of 150σ between the two stimuli. In the pseudoconditioning procedure, the tone and shock were presented the same number of times but were not paired. The GSR to the tone after training was greatest for the forward condition, was substantial for the backward condition, and was minimal for the pseudoconditioning procedure. It seems possible that backward conditioning can occur when the response is one of fear or arousal but not when the response is a muscular movement. The utility of fear arises when the organism has gotten into a dangerous situation and survived. The cue might well be the one present, during or even after the arousal of fear, when the organism is looking around to see what might have signaled the presence of the dangerous situation.

In delayed conditioning, the CS is continued in the interval between the onset of the CS and the onset of the US, and the results are somewhat different and more variable than is the case with trace conditioning. Hartman and Grant (1962) conditioned the eyeblink in a discrimination situation in which only one of two CSs was followed by the US. They report the best conditioning to the positive stimulus at about 600σ and the best discrimination at about 800σ, results that are not too different from similar studies with trace conditioning. Gerall and Woodward (1958) conditioned human pupil dilation and obtained the best results with a CS-US interval of $1,500\sigma$. Smaller pupil changes occurred with intervals of 125σ, 500σ, and $2,500\sigma$, but all of these showed conditioning when compared to a group that had the stimuli unpaired. Kimmel and Pennypacker (1963) obtained optimal GSR conditioning using shock as the US in human subjects when the delay interval was $1,000\sigma$. The best discrimination occurred at $2,000\sigma$. Fish conditioned with an illumination change as CS and shock as US showed best conditioning at $2,000\sigma$ CS-US interval, and appreciable conditioning at other intervals ranging from 500σ to $4,000\sigma$ (Noble, Gruender, and Meyer, 1959). Ross (1961) paired an illumination change with shock in human subjects. To measure the effect, he delivered a puff of air to the cornea and noted the amplitude of the blink. He found the best conditioning at $2,000\sigma$ and $5,000\sigma$, appreciable conditioning at $10,000\sigma$, but little or none at 500σ, the optimal interval in trace conditioning. Thus classical delayed conditioning involving a variety of responses and subjects shows optimal intervals ranging from 600σ to $5,000\sigma$, sometimes shows little conditioning at 500σ, and frequently shows substantial conditioning at intervals longer than the $2,250\sigma$, regarded as beyond the limit of association in classical trace conditioning. Thus, the continued presence of the CS appears to bridge the time gap and allow association over longer intervals.

Even longer intervals can be used in avoidance conditioning. In fact, the shorter intervals of classical conditioning are frequently ineffective. For example, Schwartz (1958) obtained better learning of a shuttlebox response in rats with a six second delay between the CS and the shock than he did with a three second delay. Low and Low (1962) used intervals of two, four, six, eight, and 10 seconds in a similar study and obtained better learning the longer the interval. Beyond this range, Brush, Brush, and Solomon (1955) and Church, Brush, and Solomon (1956) found very little difference in the shuttlebox performance of dogs with intervals ranging from five to 40 seconds. Figure 4.9 shows the results of Brush, Brush, and Solomon (1955) compared with those of Kamin (1954). These studies, carried out in the same laboratory, are probably sufficiently similar to permit the conclusion that the differences are attributable to differences between the trace procedure (Kamin) and the delayed procedure (Brush, Brush, and Solomon). The fact that Kamin's animals received a greater number of shocks before reaching criterion as the interval was increased means that they were learning less efficiently to jump the barrier.

The usual interpretation of CS-US interval, as it affects association, is that there is a brief latency period after the onset of the stimulus before it has its full effect on the organism. Therefore, the fact that conditioning is better when the interval is about 500σ than when the two stimuli are presented simultaneously is attributed to the likelihood that the CS has reached its maximum effect after this length of time. The decrease in effectiveness of a CS as the interval is lengthened beyond 500σ is attributed to a generally decaying trace of the stimulus; this means a progressively less efficient trace-US interaction when the US is presented. The delayed procedure is presumed to maintain an active process representing the CS and thus bridges longer intervals such as those used in the Brush, Brush, and Solomon study.

That longer optimal intervals are obtained in avoidance conditioning than are obtained in classical conditioning might be explained by the

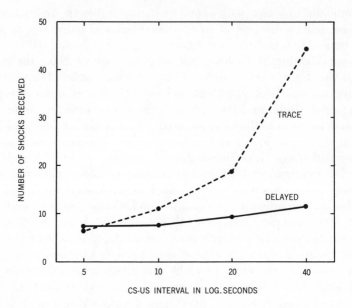

Figure 4.9

Comparison between the numbers of shocks received before reaching criterion performance by dogs trained to jump to avoid shock under (1) trace and (2) delayed-conditioning procedures. (These results are replotted from Kamin, 1954, and Brush, Brush, and Solomon, 1955. Copyright 1955 by The American Psychological Association and reproduced by permission.)

fact that the latency of a complex instrumental response, such as a dog jumping over a barrier in a shuttlebox, is much longer than the latency of an eyeblink. Therefore, a longer CS-US interval is required for the jumping response to occur in anticipation of the shock.

DELAY OF REWARD

A significant time interval in selective learning through reinforcement is the interval between the occurrence of the response and the appearance of the reward. One of the earliest studies of this variable showed no difference in learning between a condition in which the reward was immediately available and one in which it was delayed for 30 seconds. Watson (1917) trained rats to dig through sawdust to find a hole which permitted access to a food chamber. In the chamber, there was a food cup covered by a perforated lid. In the immediate-reward condition, the animal was allowed to eat as soon as it reached the chamber. In another group, the lid was removed 30 seconds after the animal reached the food chamber. Both groups learned rapidly, and there were no differences between them.

Later studies found differences in learning with differences in delay of reward, and Watson's results were accounted for on the basis of the likelihood that the smell of the food through the perforations in the lid served as a secondary reinforcement of the response. In studies in which some of the sources of secondary reinforcement were removed, a sharp gradient of reward was found indicating that the longer the reward is delayed, the slower is the learning. For example, in two studies by Perin (1943a, b) it was estimated that no learning would occur if the reward was delayed somewhere between 14 and 44 seconds. Both of these studies were run in situations in which a lever could be presented to the animal, the lever withdrawn when a response occurred, and the delivery of the reward delayed at will. In a simple lever-pressing situation, some learning occurred with a 10 second delay, but none apparently occurred with a 30 second delay. In another situation in which the animal was required to learn whether to push the lever to the left or right, the obtained curves extrapolate to zero learning at 34–44 seconds.

A typical curve showing the relation of rate of learning to the delay of reward is that in Figure 4.10 obtained by Grice (1948). He trained animals to choose either a black or white stimulus, and then delayed the animals in a gray chamber before admitting them to gray goal boxes. In this way the secondary reinforcing properties of the black and white stimuli were acquired under the same delay of reinforcement as the response itself. With this control of secondary reinforcement, all animals learned if the delay was two seconds or less, but two of 10 animals failed to learn with a five second delay and three of five failed to learn with a 10 second delay. The plot in Figure 4.10 is of medians of the number of trials to learn, and the dashed portion of the curve indicates that some animals failed to learn within the time allowed by the patience of the experimenter. A group that had black and white goal boxes, thus permitting acquisition of secondary reinforcement without the delay, learned in 155 trials with a five second delay between the response and access to the goal box.

Findings such as those of Grice suggest that the gradient of reward might be largely a matter of the delay between a relevant stimulus and the reward rather than between the response and the reward. This suggestion leads to experiments such as that of Bersh (1951), the results of which are shown in Figure 4.11. In this study, different values of secondary reinforcement were set up by pairing a light with the delivery of food pellets to hungry animals. Bersh used a delayed conditioning procedure in varying the CS-reinforcement interval. For different groups

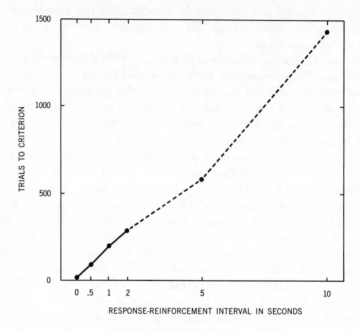

Figure 4.10

Effect of delay of reinforcement on the number of trials to meet the criterion of learning in a black-white discrimination problem. (Data are from Grice, 1948. Copyright 1948 by The American Psychological Association and reproduced by permission.)

the light came on 10, 4, 2, 1, .5, or 0 seconds before the delivery of food and remained on for two seconds after the pellet was delivered. The acquired reinforcement value of the light was then tested by introducing a lever which produced a one second light when pressed. The animals were placed in the box for 45 minutes on each of two successive days. Figure 4.11 is a plot of the median numbers of presses of the lever each group produced for no other reward than the light. In a similar study, Jenkins (1950) demonstrated a small degree of secondary reinforcement when the delay was either 27 or 81 seconds.

On the basis of results such as these, it appears possible that there is no gradient of primary reward. To be effective, reward, either primary or secondary, must be immediate. Learning occurs when there is a time gap between the response and the reward because, as suggested by Miller (1951), previously neutral stimuli acquire secondary reinforcement value and thus bridge the time gap.

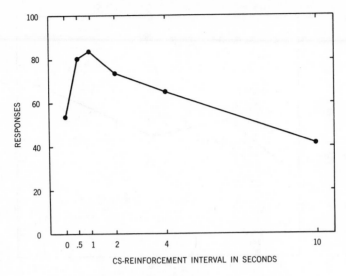

Figure 4.11

The strength of secondary reinforcement acquired at different delay intervals between the CS and the reinforcement, measured in terms of the number of responses performed to produce the CS in two 45-minute periods of two days. (Adapted from Bersh, 1951. Copyright 1951 by The American Psychological Association and reproduced by permission.)

INTERTRIAL INTERVAL AND THE CONSOLIDATION HYPOTHESIS

A significant time interval in all learning is the time between two learning trials, or the time between a learning trial and some test of the amount of learning. There are a great many studies of learning in which trials are closely spaced, usually referred to as *massed practice*, for one group, and for another group are more widely spaced, usually called *spaced practice*. It is a common finding that learning progresses more rapidly with spaced practice than with massed practice. Unfortunately, there are usually only two degrees of spacing and little agreement on how much time must separate trials to constitute the most efficient conditions of learning.

In studies in which more than two intervals between trials have been used, no simple increase in the efficiency of learning arose from increases in the amount of time between trials. For example, in a study of intertrial interval in eyelid conditioning, Spence and Norris (1950) gave four groups of human subjects 100 classical conditioning trials with

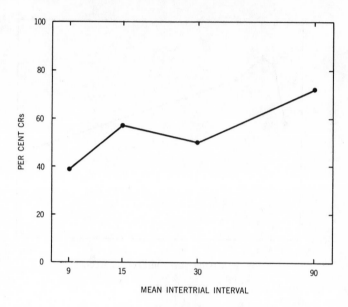

Figure 4.12

Curve showing differences in conditioning resulting from different intervals between conditioning trials. The intervals were variable, ranging from 6–12, 10–20, 20–40, and 60–120, and are plotted at the arithmetic mean value. The data are the percent CRs in the last 40 of 100 trials. (Adapted from Spence, and Norris, 1950. Copyright 1950 by The American Psychological Association and reproduced by permission.)

variable intertrial intervals with means of 9, 15, 30, and 90 seconds for the various groups. Figure 4.12 shows that it is generally true that the longer the intertrial interval the more effective is the same number of trials, but performance was somewhat better at 15 seconds than at 30. That such findings might not be accidental can be seen in a study by Kamin (1963) in which he gave rats 25 training trials in which they avoided shock in a shuttle box. He then gave them another block of 25 trials with varying amounts of time between the two blocks of trials. Figure 4.13 shows that the performance of the animals in the second block was significantly poor when either one or six hours intervened. From the data of these two studies, and others, it is possible only to generalize that some complex process is occurring during a significant interval after a single practice trial or after a series of trials, and that either a test or further training is likely to be affected by this process.

A common speculation as to the nature of that process is that an

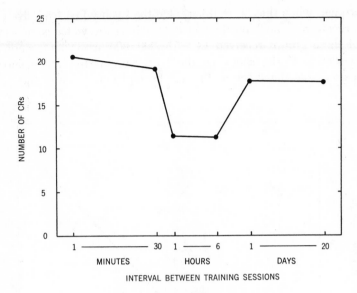

Figure 4.13

Curve showing the number of conditioned responses in a second training session depending upon the amount of time between the first and the second session. (Data drawn from Kamin, 1963. Copyright 1963 by The American Psychological Association and reproduced by permission.)

effective stimulus or a bit of behavior sets up an active neural process that continues for a significant period of time after the stimulus has been removed or the response has ceased. Such a process is called a *perseverative stimulus trace* or a *perseverative memory trace*. It is a further speculation that perseveration is necessary to produce the semipermanent structural changes on which the long-term effects of practice, and thus learning and memory, depend. Perseveration of the trace is said to produce *consolidation* of the semipermanent *memory trace*.

There is a large number of studies based on this hypothesis. They take the general form of providing a given amount of training or experience, then subjecting the organism to some procedure such as the application of electroconvulsive shock (*ECS*) which is presumed to disrupt the perseverative consolidation process. By varying the interval between the practice and the application of *ECS*, differing amounts of permanent memory are thought to be "laid down" before the disruption prevents further consolidation. The results of one of many such studies are shown in Figure 4.14. These are results from a study by King (1965). He trained six groups of animals to run down a passage to a water compartment when they were thirsty. On the twenty-first trial, five of the groups received a shock on the feet on reaching the water compartment. Four of these groups received *ECS* 75, 300, 900, or 3,600 seconds after the experience of the shock on the feet. King tested for memory of the experience of the shock on the feet by replacing them in the runway

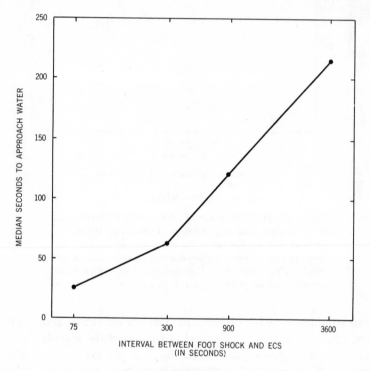

Figure 4.14

Effect of interval between experience of shock on the feet and electroconvulsive shock (ECS) on the tendency to return to the water compartment in which the foot shock was received. (Data drawn from King, 1965. Copyright 1965 by The American Psychological Association. Reproduced by permission of the author and publisher.)

and measuring how long it took them to return to the water compartment. In Figure 4.14 it is apparent that the animals who were subjected to *ECS* 75 seconds after the experience of the foot shock returned rather quickly, as if they did not remember being shocked. If the *ECS* was delayed longer, the animals took longer to return until, at an interval of 3,600 seconds (one hour), the animals took an average of about 234 seconds to return. Since a group that was shocked but did not have *ECS* took about 238 seconds, it is presumed that a delay of one hour was sufficient, in this case, to permit consolidation of the memory of the experience. A sixth group that was given *ECS*, but was not shocked on the feet, took only 10 seconds to return to the water compartment.

A number of other procedures have also been employed either to facilitate the trace or to disrupt it and prevent consolidation. For example, McGaugh, Westbrook, and Thomson (1962) and Breen and McGaugh (1961) report facilitation of learning through injection of drugs. The assumption is that the drugs produce, in some manner, a more vigorous perseverative trace and thus greater learning. On the other hand, Pearlman, Sharpless, and Jarvik (1961) used other drugs to disrupt the trace. They report that ether was effective only if administered very quickly after training. Pentobarbital was somewhat more effective, giving some evidence of trace disruption when applied as much as 10 minutes after the learning. Pentylenetetrazol appeared to disrupt the trace completely when administered within eight hours, and showed some effect when administered four days later.

While the study by King and a number of others like it seem to have established that there is a perseverative consolidation process that is necessary for the storage of permanent memory, many psychologists feel that the effects of *ECS* and drugs can be explained in other ways. For example, Coons and Miller (1960) have suggested that most of the effects of *ECS* can be accounted for on the basis that *ECS* constitutes an unpleasant experience and that the animal learns to avoid the situation that led to it. Lewis and Maher (1965) review the literature and conclude that *ECS* produces an inhibition which becomes conditioned to the *ECS* situation and prevents performance of the response. Glickman (1961), on the other hand, reviews the literature and concludes that the over-all weight of the evidence favors some mechanism of consolidation in spite of alternative interpretations of individual experiments.

TRANSFER OF TRAINING

For learning to be useful to the learner, he must be able to transfer his learning from the training situation to other situations. The problem of transfer of training has given rise to three primary areas of laboratory research. The term *stimulus generalization* refers to the fact that a given response can be elicited to some degree by a range of similar stimuli. *Response generalization* is a term that applies to the fact that the same stimulus can be shown to produce a range of responses, either within a single trial or between trials depending on the nature of the situation. The concept of generalization is inseparable from the capacity of the organism to discriminate between similar stimuli and responses. Thus the third basic concept of transfer of training is that of *discrimination*. Research on these three concepts will be discussed in turn.

STIMULUS GENERALIZATION

While the term applies to the capacity of a range of stimuli to produce unconditioned as well as conditioned responses, demonstrations of stimulus generalization usually proceed by first establishing the capacity of a stimulus to elicit the response in question through conditioning, and then testing the capacity of other stimuli to produce some aspect of that response. A demonstration of the generalization of a conditioned response is shown in Figure 4.15. In two studies, Hovland (1937a, b; Hull, 1943) measured generalization to differences in pitch and loudness.

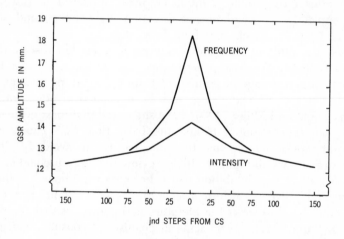

Figure 4.15

Generalization gradients for tonal frequency and intensity, both measured in terms of the number of just noticeable differences (jnd) in pitch or intensity from CS. The response measured is the amplitude of the galvanic skin response (GSR). (The data are from Hovland, 1937a. Copyright 1937 by The Journal Press. The drawing is adapted from Figures 42 and 43 of Principles of Behavior *by C. L. Hull. Copyright 1943 by D. Appleton-Century Co. Reprinted by permission of Appleton-Century-Crofts.)*

He first paired a tone with shock in human subjects, and conditioned the galvanic skin response to the tone. Then he tested by presenting tones that differed from the CS by 25, 50, or 75 *jnd's*. (A *jnd* is a "just noticeable difference" and is obtained by a psychophysical method that involves finding a tone that can just be distinguished as being different from a reference tone. It is assumed that *jnd's* are psychologically equal.) The figure is plotted to show that either increasing or decreasing the pitch produced a decrease in the amplitude of the *GSR*; the greater the change, the less *GSR*. In the case of intensity generalization, the decrease in *GSR* with differences in intensity from the original *CS* was relatively small, even over a wider range of *jnd's* in intensity. There is a further complication in testing for intensity generalization. In the Hovland study, the more intense the test stimulus, quite independent of the generalization problem, the greater the *GSR*. The curve plotted in Figure 4.15 is composed by combining subjects who were tested with more intense stimuli than the original *CS* with subjects who were tested with stimuli which are less intense. Thus the curve is assumed to reflect only the generalization effect. The symmetry of the two curves in the figure is produced by plotting the same data twice, once in each direction from the training stimulus. Thus it represents a combination of empirical fact and assumptions concerning the nature of generalization.

This mixture of reasonable fiction and actual fact arises from both logical and technical difficulties in producing an unambiguous demonstration of stimulus generalization. Logically, no two stimuli can ever be absolutely identical. Therefore, there is some problem involved in explaining how learning takes place at all, since each presentation of a stimulus involves a "new stimulus." To say that stimuli are "similar" is of little help until the nature of similarity is specified. Technically, the demonstration of generalization is difficult because great time and effort are usually expended in establishing the response. At the first test with a "similar" stimulus, a response can be measured, but no further uncomplicated tests can be made. On the first test, the response must be either reinforced, thus producing learning in the presence of that stimulus, or not reinforced, thus producing extinction to that stimulus. The inefficiency of extensive training followed by a single test, along with the necessity for a very large number of tests to establish the precise form of a generalization curve, has so far prohibited an unambiguous empirical solution.

What one means by "similarity" constitutes a problem. One possibility is to regard stimuli as being similar or equivalent to the extent to which they produce the same response. This is the "stimulus equivalence" position. Thus one cannot presume to predict generalization; one can only try stimuli and classify stimuli according to whether some degree of the response occurs. This position not only does not allow the prediction of generalization, but does not permit one to plot a generalization gradient, for there is no scale against which the amount of the response can be plotted. To plot a gradient of stimulus generalization, it is necessary to make some assumption about the similarity of stimuli. The two most common "independent" definitions of similarity involve the use of either a physical scale or a psychological scale as the dimensions in terms of which the stimuli are arranged. Thus Hovland might have used the physical frequency of the tone and plotted the magnitude of the GSR response against vibrations per second. Problems arise, however, from this solution. Blackwell and Schlosberg (1943) demonstrated that the amount of generalization to a tone one octave away from the training tone produced a greater tendency to respond than did tones on either side of it. Thus, with a training tone of 10,000 cps, rats responded as if a tone of 5,000 cps was more similar than tones of 8,000 or 7,000 cps. Furthermore, generalization may occur between stimuli for which there is no underlying physical dimension. In many learning situations, for example, one might wish to predict the degree of generalization from one stimulus to another where the stimuli do not share a relevant physical dimension. In such cases, generalization must be measured along some psychological dimension, such as similarity in meaning or similarity in sound, that must be measured independently from the response under study. Even this solution poses difficulties. Guttman and Kalish (1956) trained pigeons to peck at a key illuminated by a color produced by a relatively narrow band of wavelengths and then tested for generalization to other wavelengths. When the generalization curve obtained in this way was compared to a curve showing the discriminability of the various wavelengths, it was concluded that the pigeons were generalizing in response to the physical properties of the stimulus (such as frequency) rather than the psychological properties (such as *jnd's*). The implication of this conclusion has been challenged, however, by Shepard (1965), who derived the Guttman and Kalish generalization gradient from the discrimination function, thus implying that the generalization function and the discrimination function had a common origin. Furthermore, Kalish (1958) carried out a similar study with human subjects and found generalization to conform to the psychological scale rather than the physical one. Thus it is not necessarily true that a scale of "similarity" obtained with one set of measuring techniques will define the dimension the organism responds to in another.

Explanations of generalization take the form of specifying what it is that is common to the generalized response and the scale of similarity against which it is plotted (such as the *jnd* scale in Figure 4.15). The three most common explanations are phrased in terms of (1) an underlying psychological scale, (2) common stimulus elements, or (3) mediation by some common association. In Hovland's study, it was assumed that the independent measurement of difference thresholds of pitch reflected an underlying dimension of similarity in pitch, and that the

GSR response reflected this same scale. According to the second explanation, stimuli are composed of large numbers of small, unitary elements. The *CS* is composed of one large set of elements, and the amount of generalization is thought to be determined by the proportion of this set of elements that occurs in a test stimulus. Explanation in terms of mediation suggests that the connection between stimulus and response is not direct, but is rather mediated by some response with which both have been associated. All three explanations are theoretical and define "similarity" in terms of an underlying property that is assumed to be common to both sets of measurements (e.g., *jnd's* and *GSR*).

The complexities of the problems of stimulus generalization have produced a great many experiments and theoretical arguments. An excellent summary of the experiments and the theoretical issues underlying them may be found in Kimble (1961).

RESPONSE GENERALIZATION

Similarity between responses poses an even more difficult problem than that of similarity between stimuli. It is clear that when one response is conditioned to a stimulus, other responses are associated to some degree—but a problem arises in trying to establish a dimension of response similarity. No simple solution to the problem has been developed. Possibly the most useful idea is Hull's (1943) concept of *habit-family hierarchy*. He conceived the organism as being born with a family of responses that are more likely than others to occur and to produce satisfaction when a biological need arises. He thought of these responses as being arranged in a hierarchy in terms of their probability of occurrence. If one analyzes the behavior of a newborn pup, for example, the sequence of responses that lead to nursing for the first time can be thought of as being composed of a number of distinguishable responses involving movements of the forelegs, hind legs, body, and mouth. They vary in likelihood of occurrence, but they are not random. When a pup first nurses successfully, according to Hull, the original hierarchy of responses is reordered in terms of their probability of occurrence—with those responses that led to reinforcement increasing in probability and those that did not lead to reinforcement decreasing in probability. Thus in any given situation, the responses that will occur can be ordered in terms of their probability of occurrence, the ordering described as a hierarchy, and the heirarchy rearranged on the basis of the reinforcement experience. This conception of response generalization is very similar to the stimulus-equivalence conception of stimulus generalization, in that no underlying "dimension of similarity" is identified with either.

DISCRIMINATION

Generalization implies discrimination. A difference in response must be based on a perceived difference in stimulus. Sometimes generalization is described as a failure to discriminate. However, the human subjects in Hovland's experiment shown in Figure 4.15 were certainly able to discriminate between the different pitches, even though they responded to pitches different from the training pitch. Therefore, the subjects could discriminate at one level (by detecting just noticeable differences in pitch) and failed to discriminate at another level (by giving a GSR to a pitch other than the training pitch).

In discrimination learning, one stimulus is usually followed by reward and another stimulus followed by nonreward. For example, a rat might be rewarded for choosing a dark gray alley and not rewarded for choosing an alley painted a lighter shade of gray. Under these circumstances, the animal will show learning by coming to choose the dark alley most, if not all, of the time.

There are two prominent approaches to the explanation of discrimination learning. In one, the tendency to respond to the dark gray is explained by the accumulation of habit strength through reinforcement, while the tendency to respond to the light gray stimulus is said to be extinguished through nonreinforcement. Both tendencies are considered to be generalized, but the performance comes to a high level when the difference in habit strength to the light and the dark stimuli is sufficiently great that discrimination is established.

The other prominent explanation is that an animal in a discrimination situation learns a *relation* between the stimuli, and, in the example, comes to choose the *darker* of the pair. This leads to the expectation that an animal trained in the manner described will choose the darker of a new pair of stimuli, thus transposing the relationship he has learned from the original stimuli. If the animal is asked to choose between the dark stimulus that has previously led to reward and a very much darker stimulus, he will be expected to respond to the relation of the stimuli rather than to their absolute properties, and to choose the very much darker stimulus. This result has been observed and is called the *transposition phenomenon*. In spite of the apparent contradiction between these results and an explanation in terms of habit tendencies with respect to absolute properties of the stimuli, an explanation can be and has been developed by Spence (1937). For an account of the theoretical issues involved in explanations of transposition, and a review of the relevant experimental studies, see Kimble (1961, pp. 378ff.).

ELIMINATION OF LEARNED RESPONSES

EXPERIMENTAL EXTINCTION

If, after a CR is established, a CS is repeatedly presented alone and is not followed by the US, the usual result is a gradual reduction in the amplitude of the CR. The term *experimental extinction* was originally used to refer to the procedure of omitting the US and thus presenting the CS alone. However, in general usage, the term has gradually come to refer to the disappearance of the CR through a variety of procedures other than the omission of the US. In selective learning through reinforcement, experimental extinction refers to the procedure of omitting the reward and also to the disappearance of the response. Thus the term "experimental extinction" is used both as a name for procedures and as a name for the results of those procedures.

The course of experimental extinction of a classical conditioned response may be seen in Figure 4.16. These data are taken from a study by Hovland. The GSR response had been conditioned to a tone by pairing the tone with a shock to the wrists of human subjects. The figure is a plot of the magnitude of the GSR as a percentage of the amplitude on the first extinction trial. The response on this first trial occurs, of course, before the subject has experienced the first omission of the shock and therefore represents the amplitude at the end of training. The decrease in the amplitude of response occurs quite abruptly in this experiment and appears to reflect the disappearance of the effects of training after as few as five trials of experimental extinction. Very similar curves can be obtained in selective learning when, after a period of training, the reward is omitted.

There are a number of empirical phenomena associated with the process of experimental extinction that make quite clear that while experimental extinction as a *procedure* is quite simple, it is quite complex as a *process*.

AMOUNT OF TRAINING

It is generally true that the greater the amount of training, the stronger the habit, and the greater the resistance to extinction. This principle is so widely accepted that the number of trials to extinguish a response is taken as the measure of the strength of the habit. For example, in Figure 4.2 the number of trials to extinction is used as a measure of the amount of habit strength developed through different numbers in reinforcements (Harris and Nygaard, 1961). Furthermore, some degree of "overtraining" produced by continuing reinforcement beyond the point at which the animals meet the criterion of learning

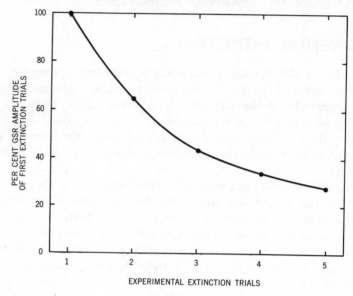

Figure 4.16

The course of experimental extinction of a conditioned GSR response in human subjects. The amplitude of the GSR on the first trial of experimental extinction is taken as 100 percent, and the amplitudes of subsequent responses are expressed as percentages of that amount. (The figure is replotted from Figure 57 of Principles of Behavior *by C. L. Hull. Copyright 1943 by D. Appleton-Century Co. Reprinted by permission of Appleton-Century-Crofts.)*

produces an increase in resistance to extinction. Mackintosh (1963), among others, reports such a result. However, the opposite result may be obtained if the problem is simple and the overtraining extended. For example, Ison (1962) trained hungry rats in an extremely simple problem, running down a straight alley to obtain food. The problem is so simple that animals learn to run at near maximum speed in a very few trials—less than the 10 trials Ison used as a minimum. He trained six groups which had 10, 20, 40, 60, 80, or 100 reinforced trials before experimental extinction was instituted by removal of the reward. He used several different criteria for extinction, but the most dramatic results appeared with a criterion that the animal not enter the box in 120 seconds. These results are plotted in Figure 4.17, where it is clear that the greater the number of reinforcements, the *faster* extinction occurred. These results are consistent with the results shown in Figures 4.3 and 4.4

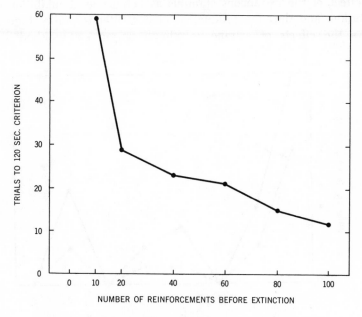

Figure 4.17

Decrease in resistance to extinction with overlearning. Ison (1962) gave varying numbers of reinforced responses in a simple runway before beginning extinction. (Adapted from Ison, 1962. Copyright 1962 by The American Psychological Association and reproduced by permission.)

which indicate that response strength may rise and fall with continued reinforcement.

FORGETTING

There is general agreement that most of the responses conditioned in the laboratory are not forgotten, even over long periods of time. The author once conditioned leg flexion in a hunting dog and then gave the dog to a farmer. Two years later the dog was tested and showed no forgetting of the response. Kimble (1961) lists a number of reports showing little if any forgetting of a variety of responses in a number of different organisms.

DISINHIBITION

If an extraneous stimulus is introduced during the experimental extinction procedure, the result is frequently one of an increase in the response on that trial. Pavlov (1927) thought of the process of experimental extinction as being an inhibition of the response, and thought of the effect of the extraneous stimulus as being one of inhibition of the inhibition, and thus the production of a greater response. Figure 4.18 shows the effects of extraneous stimuli on an extinguished salivary

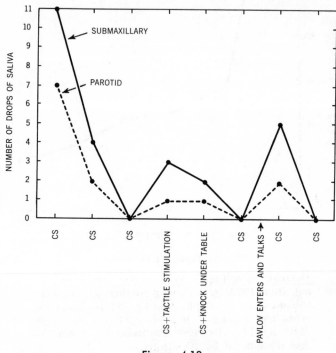

Figure 4.18

Extinction and disinhibition of a conditioned salivary response in a dog. Salivary response was trained to the sight of meat powder, and the response was measured in terms of the drops of saliva from two glands, the submaxillary and the parotid. After extinction, the response reappeared with tactile stimulation, a knock on the table, and after Professor Pavlov had entered the room and talked between trials. (Figure is redrawn by I. P. Pavlov, Conditioned Reflexes, *1927 [Clarendon Press, Oxford], by permission.)*

response. Zavadsky, a student of Pavlov's, conditioned a dog to salivate using the sight and smell of the food powder as the CS, and ingestion of the food as the US. Then he extinguished the response quickly by presenting the sight of the meat powder at a distance for one minute periods every five minutes. The response was measured in terms of the number of drops of saliva secreted from each of two fistulated salivary glands, the submaxillary and the parotid. After the response in both glands had extinguished, disinhibition was produced first by applying tactile stimulation along with the sight of the meat powder and then by knocking on the table when the powder was presented. The extraneous stimuli produced salivation in both glands. After one more trial with the CS alone, which did not elicit a response, Professor Pavlov entered the room and talked for two minutes. After he did, the meat powder was again presented at a distance and appreciable salivation occurred.

SPONTANEOUS RECOVERY

An extinguished conditioned response sometimes reappears spontaneously after a lapse of time. Figure 4.19 shows spontaneous recovery of a salivary response in one of Pavlov's dogs (1927) after a lapse of

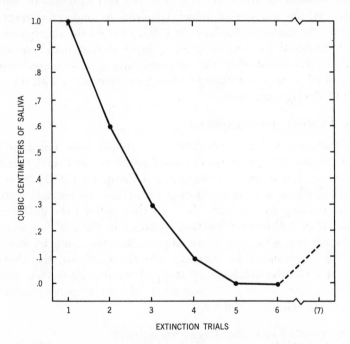

Figure 4.19

Spontaneous recovery of a conditioned salivary response. The sight of meat powder without ingestion extinguished within six trials. After a two hour period, the sight of meat powder again elicited a significant salivary response. (Figure is redrawn from I. P. Pavlov, Conditioned Reflexes, 1927 [Clarendon Press, Oxford], by permission.)

two hours in which the dog had been left alone. While the response in the figure recovered only about 15 percent of the original strength, much larger amounts of spontaneous recovery are not uncommon. Ellson (1938), for example, varied the amount of time between the end of experimental extinction and the test for spontaneous recovery of a lever-pressing response in rats and found a steadily increasing amount of spontaneous recovery the longer the interval. After about three hours, the response recovered to slightly less than 50 percent of the original response strength. If the extinction procedure is continued for a sufficient number of trials after the response has disappeared, no spontaneous recovery will occur. This procedure is sometimes referred to as "below-zero" extinction.

AMOUNT OF EFFORT

The number of trials to extinguish the response can be shown to decrease as the amount of effort required to make the response is increased. For example, Applezweig (1951) varied the number of grams pressure required for rats to press a lever during both learning and extinction. He found that the response strength increased with the amount of effort required during training, but decreased with the amount of weight during extinction.

PUNISHMENT FOR RESPONDING

If punishment for responding is combined with omission of the US or omission of the reward, the usual result is rapid disappearance of the response. For example, Seligman and Campbell (1965) trained rats to avoid shock in a runway. During extinction the animals were punished for running by receiving shock as they entered the goal box. Several intensities and several durations of shock in the goal box were used. They found just what one might expect, that the more intense or the longer the punishment for running into the goal box, the slower the animals ran and the quicker they stopped running altogether. However, punishment can produce enhancement of the response under some conditions, as will be noted later.

CONDITIONS PRODUCING GREAT RESISTANCE TO EXTINCTION

There are several training procedures which produce very persistent and almost intractable responding. Avoidance-conditioning procedures often produce learning and high resistance to extinction in a very few trials. For example, in a standard procedure used with dogs, a tone might be used as a CS, and the response elicited by a shock on the forepaw. If the apparatus is designed to permit the dog to avoid the shock altogether by lifting his paw before the shock appears, avoidance may be established in as few as two or three trials. It may then persist beyond the patience of the experimenter (possibly 500 trials) without noticeable evidence of extinction, even though the shock is no longer given no matter what the animal does. Punishment of an avoidance response, under certain conditions, also leads to persistence of responding. The contrast between this effect of punishment and the more usual effect of hastening extinction is referred to as the punishment paradox. This problem is discussed on page 80 in a general treatment of the reinforcing effects of punishment. High resistance to extinction can be produced by partial or intermittent reinforcement in contrast to 100 percent reinforcement of the response. (This problem is discussed in the next chapter, Operant Conditioning.)

EXPLANATIONS OF EXPERIMENTAL EXTINCTION

There is a wide range of explanations that could be and have been offered for the gradual disappearance of the response when either the US is omitted or the reward no longer follows the response.

DECREASE IN HABIT STRENGTH

If habit strength rises during reinforcement, it is a logical possibility that it falls under nonreinforcement. This possibility holds little appeal, for habit strength is defined as that component of the determiners of performance that is semipermanent and relatively immutable.

DECREASE IN INCENTIVE

The most obvious difference between acquisition and extinction is the presence during the acquisition of the US or the reward, and the absence of one or the other during extinction. If cessation of the US in conditioning is regarded as an incentive, as is the reward in selective learning, then extinction can be explained in terms of a decrease in the incentive component or term in the equation

$$P = D \times H \times I.$$

This explanation requires that with D constant during acquisition, both H and I increase with increased training. During extinction, performance decreases because the value of I decreases.

CHANGES IN DRIVE

It seems likely that D is not constant between acqusition and extinction conditions. If a noxious US is used during the acquisition phase, then its omission during extinction should produce a lower D value, possibly even a zero value of D. Unfortunately, avoidance conditioning produces high resistance to extinction, even though the US is avoided, and by this logic, the response should disappear. Omission of the reward, on the other hand, should theoretically increase the value of D. When the organism is rewarded, the reward is usually conceived as reducing the drive which is instigating the response. Omission of the reward during extinction should produce a sustained D value in place of reduction in D. Also, the removal of reward might be regarded as frustrating. Frustration might be regarded as having aversive drive properties and thus might produce an increase in D during extinction as compared to acquisition. (This possibility has been dealt with by Amsel and Roussel, 1952, and Amsel and Ward, 1954). Therefore, changes in the value of the D term in the equation might explain some of the special findings in studies of experimental extinction, but the changes do not appear to offer a plausible account of the disappearance of the response under simple experimental extinction conditions.

EXTINCTION AS THE LEARNING OF A DIFFERENT RESPONSE

In most learning situations, the growing strength of the measured response is accompanied by the disappearance of other, usually unmeasured, responses. During experimental extinction, these unmeasured responses are frequently observed to reappear. For example, in a simple runway task, the animal may be observed to explore his environment and to engage in preening and grooming behavior as well as to move eventually from the starting box to the goal box. During acquisition, these irrelevant responses disappear. In fact, most of the increase in speed of running occurs as a function of the disappearance of these irrelevant, time-consuming, and incompatible responses. During extinction they may reappear. The equation used above to describe the factors which determine performance refers only to the measured response. Consideration of the role of incompatible responses requires that performance be determined by both an expression of the value of the positive-response tendency and one expressing the strength of the incompatible response. Thus, if we use p as a notation for the positive response and i as a notation of the incompatible response, we can write an expression for performance as a function of both responses:

$$P_p = (D_p \times H_p \times I_p) - (D_i \times H_i \times I_i).$$

A great many problems arise in attempting to explain experimental extinction in this way. There is some reason to believe that all habits are influenced by all drives present, and the expression above indicates that the two drives are as incompatible as the two habits. Whether the simple algebraic form of the expression is justified or whether different, and possibly more complicated, relationships are involved is also a problem. Among the many other problems is that of the characterization of the incompatible response.

One characterization of the incompatible response is that of Hull (1943). He defined *not responding* as a response. He pointed out that the effort involved in making the response had aversive properties. He described the aftereffects of effort as a negative drive called *reactive inhibition*, which was a drive against making the response again. He thought of the dissipation of reactive inhibition as being reinforcing, and it reinforced the tendency not to respond. The habit that was built up in this way he called *conditioned inhibition*, which amounts to a learned tendency not to make the response.

The incompatible response has also been conceived of as a positive response that is simply physically incompatible with the response being measured. For example, it is a common observation in conditioning studies that the initial presentations of the CS elicit orienting responses followed by the overt response to the US. As conditioning proceeds, the orienting response tends to disappear as the conditioned response grows in strength. During extinction, the orienting response may reappear. Berlyne (1960) reviews much of the work on the orienting response, much of which was done in Russia. In this work, the orienting response is often regarded as the overt manifestation of attention.

Whatever the explanation of normal extinction, conditioned responses can be eliminated through the positive conditioning of incompatible responses. The process is called *counter conditioning* and forms the theoretical and procedural basis for some forms of behavioral therapy in clinical psychology.

CHANGES IN THE STIMULUS PATTERN BETWEEN ACQUISITION AND EXTINCTION

When the US is omitted or the reward removed during extinction, not only is the source of reinforcement removed, but important changes are made in the stimulus pattern between the conditions of acquisition and the conditions under which the response is extinguished. This fact has led to an explanation in terms of generalization. The response during extinction is regarded as a generalized response of lesser strength than the original. Efforts to manipulate the amount of stimulus change between acquisition and extinction must be evaluated in the light of the effects of stimulus variation on acquisition. Thus, for example, Voeks (1954) carried out an eyelid-conditioning study in which she exercised unusual control over stimulus variation. She had the subjects keep their eyes closed between trials and open them on signal, hold their breaths during the trial, and initiate the CS themselves by pressing two keys. All of these operations were designed to make the stimulus pattern as nearly identical as possible during the acquisition trials. Under these conditions, learning was very rapid, and about half of her subjects showed conditioning in a single trial. Walker (1948) trained two groups of rats to press a lever and then extinguished the response with one group confined to a small area before the bar and the other free in the larger compartment. The animals in the smaller area showed higher resistance to extinction. These two studies seem to justify the conclusion that under conditions of minimal stimulus change within acquisition and extinction and between the two phases of training, learning is faster and extinction is slower.

Hulicka, Capehart, and Viney (1960) deliberately manipulated the amount of change in the stimulus pattern between acquisition and extinction and found that the greater the change, the faster the extinction. Five different sets of stimuli accompanied the reinforcement during acquisition. They were the click of the food release mechanism, a light that flashed when the lever was pressed, a continuous red light near the rear of the apparatus, a continuous buzzer, and a false floor to cover the grid. Maximum responding during extinction occurred when only the reward was removed. Generally, the larger the number of stimuli that were removed along with the reward during extinction, the fewer were the responses that occurred during extinction. It therefore seems likely that the greater the difference in stimulus pattern between acquisition and extinction, the faster the extinction. It remains to be demonstrated, however, that all of the phenomena of extinction can be accounted for on the basis of change in stimulus pattern.

THE NATURE OF REINFORCEMENT

Contiguity is the oldest principle of association; reinforcement is the newest. Aristotle recognized that association occurred because of temporal and spatial contiguity. Reinforcement, as a principle of association, is a development of the twentieth century.

A reinforcer may be either positive or negative. A *positive reinforcer* may be identified as any state an organism will undertake to approach or achieve. A *negative reinforcer* may be defined as any state an organism will undertake to reduce or to avoid. These definitions describe only the *incentive function* of reinforcers. They define reinforcement in terms of approach and avoidance and say nothing about the relation of reinforcement to association or learning.

Reinforcers may also be defined in terms of their effects on associational connections. Thus a *positive reinforcer* is sometimes defined as one which produces a strengthening of a stimulus-response connection or one which increases the probability of occurrence of the response. A *negative reinforcer* may similarly be defined as one which weakens a stimulus-response connection or decreases the probability of a response.

While the incentive properties of reinforcers are denied by no one, the issue of whether reinforcers operate to strengthen associational connections is an issue of strenuous debate that is difficult to resolve. That negative reinforcers operate to weaken connections is a proposition that is widely doubted.

The terms *positive reinforcement* and *negative reinforcement* are closely associated with *reward* and *punishment.* They cannot be used interchangeably with the latter terms, however. Reward and punishment are general terms that can be used by any learning theorist regardless of his position. Thus one can be a strict behaviorist and assert that contiguity is the necessary and sufficient condition of learning and still talk about the effects of reward and punishment. The use of the word *reinforcement* implies incentive properties as a minimum, and an influence on associative strength as an additional option.

In using the terms, most reinforcement theorists assume that positive and negative reinforcers are inextricably associated. A drive state, such as hunger, is regarded as a negative reinforcer and the food reward that relieves the state is a positive reinforcer. A noxious stimulus, such as shock, is regarded as a negative reinforcer; escape from the noxious stimulus is a' positive reinforcer. An unpleasant state, such as fear, is a negative reinforcer; a reduction in fear is a positive reinforcer. Among reinforcement theorists, however, the term *negative reinforcement* is rarely used. Instead, the tendency is to use the terms *drive* or *aversive* stimulus to imply a role in the instigation of action and occasionally the term *negative incentive* to emphasize the tendency to avoid such a stimulus. Neither of these meanings implies a weakening of an associative connection. For this reason, when the term *reinforcement* is used alone, as it usually is, it refers to positive reinforcement.

REINFORCEMENT AS REDUCTION OF A BIOLOGICAL NEED

Considerable research has been devoted to an attempt to isolate the reinforcing element of the situation in which a biological need is reduced. A hungry animal sees food, consumes it, the empty stomach becomes full, and there are then changes in the chemistry of the bloodstream. Which of these phases constitute reinforcement?

One approach to this problem involves the placement of a fistula in a dog's esophagus in such a manner that either food that is swallowed can be prevented from reaching the stomach or food can be introduced directly into the stomach, bypassing the dog's mouth. Two studies, one by Kohn (1951) and one by Berkun, Kessen, and Miller (1952), are nearly identical and yield the same conclusions. In the Kohn study, animals were trained to push a panel to obtain liquid food. They were then prefed in three different ways. In one treatment, 14 cc of milk were taken by mouth but not permitted to reach the stomach. In another condition, 14 cc of milk were placed directly into the stomach. In a third condition, 14 cc of saline solution were placed directly in the stomach. Kohn then measured the rate of panel pushing for food to determine the effects of the prefeeding. After the injection of saline solution in the stomach, the rate of panel pushing for liquid food was about 13 pushes a minute, but after milk had been injected in the stomach, the rate was a little over seven responses a minute. These results seem to mean that even when the consummatory response had been bypassed, some reinforcement had occurred. However, when prefeeding consisted of the animal consuming milk which did not reach the stomach, the rate of panel pushing was only a little over 5.5 responses a minute. This result seems to indicate that the consumption of the milk had been reinforcing even though the biological need had not been reduced. The Berkun, Kessen, and Miller study yielded almost identical results when the amount of food, rather than the rate of instrumental responding, was taken as the measure.

Miller and Kessen (1952) extended this fistulation and feeding procedure to a T-maze learning situation. They wished to determine if the animals could discriminate between the various treatments and which treatment would be regarded by the animal as preferable or most reinforcing. If an animal made an incorrect choice, it received 14 cc of saline solution directly in the stomach. Three different rewards were offered different groups. Animals that received milk in the mouth, even though it did not reach the stomach, learned to choose the milk side quickly. Thus milk in the mouth was reinforcing. However, injecting milk in the stomach takes considerable time and a direct comparison between milk in the mouth and milk in the stomach would be complicated by differential delay of reward. Therefore, they ran a group that received milk in the stomach for a correct choice and a group that received milk in the mouth seven minutes and 35 seconds after the choice. Both groups were able to discriminate and learned the problem. The group receiving delayed milk in the mouth performed slightly better than the group receiving milk in the stomach. Thus both the consummatory process alone and the reduction of the biological need without consumption appear to be reinforcing.

Both the consummatory process and food in the stomach were bypassed by Coppock and Chambers (1954) and Chambers (1956a, b). They injected glucose directly into the bloodstream in rabbits as reinforcement for head turning. The animals showed a preference for glucose rather than xylose injected into the bloodstream, and the preference was greater when they were hungry. Thus, this study taken with the previous studies appears to establish that direct injection, stomach loading, and food consumption are all independently reinforcing.

Sheffield and Roby (1950) demonstrated that animals would learn to choose the correct side of a T maze when the reward was sweet tasting but nonnutritive saccharine. Sheffield, Wulff, and Backer (1951) demonstrated that male rats would learn to run a straight alley to reach a female even though copulation was interrupted before ejaculation. Both studies can be interpreted as demonstrating that a stimulus *increase* can serve as a reinforcement in contradiction to the requirement of a reduction in either stimulation or need.

A great variety of other stimuli, objects, and conditions have been shown to be reinforcing that cannot easily be related to biological needs. Animals will perform a great variety of responses for a reward that consists of a pulse of electrical current to some portions of the brain tissue delivered through implanted electrodes (Olds and Milner, 1954; Olds, 1956). These studies are discussed in more detail in Butter (pending). Harlow (1950) and Harlow, Harlow, and Meyers (1950) have shown that monkeys will learn to unlock a hasp on the cage with no extraneous motivation or reward. Butler (1954) has demonstrated that an isolated monkey will work hard for no other reward than the chance to explore a visual environment through a window, and will learn a discrimination for visual exploration (1953) and auditory stimulation (1957). Montgomery (1954) showed that rats would learn to choose an arm of a single-choice-point maze to attain an opportunity to explore a complex environment in preference to a simple one. Kish and Barnes (1961) showed that mice prefer a movable lever to an unmovable one. Miles (1958) found that kittens would learn a Y maze to reach a toy or a room to explore almost as fast as they would learn it for food when hungry. Pubols (1962) offered animals a choice between a fixed or a variable delay of reward and found a preference for the variable delay. Studies by Kish (1955), Forgays and Levin (1958, 1959), Robinson (1961), and Levin and Forgays (1960) show that under appropriate conditions mice will work to turn a light on or off. These studies suggest that stimulus change is reinforcing.

EXPLANATIONS OF REINFORCEMENT

A basic explanation of the nature of reinforcement is that it is a reduction of a biological need. This need-reduction theory is generally identified with Hull (1943, 1952), who specified that the reduction in a stimulus that is characteristic of a biological need is what actually constitutes reinforcement. This position can be retained, even in the light of the above evidence in the foregoing paragraph, if one appeals to secondary reinforcement or acquired reward value. Thus, all of the stimuli closely associated with actual need reduction can acquire reinforcing properties, and instances of reinforcement without reduction in a biological need can be accounted for in terms of the presence of the secondary reinforcers. If reinforcement has no obvious connection with hunger, thirst, fear, or sexual needs, then additional drives or needs can be postulated. Thus, it is possible to talk of a need to explore or a need for stimulus change. In this vein, it can be shown that the longer Butler's monkeys are isolated, within limits, the harder they will work to earn a chance to look at electric trains or other monkeys. Likewise, Kish and Baron (1962) showed that the lever-pressing behavior of mice to turn lights on and off could be controlled to a degree by the character of a pre-exposure period, dark or light, changing or unchanging.

An alternative to a need-reduction theory of reinforcement is a stimulus-reduction theory. Miller (1951) argues that any strong stimulus is drive producing and that the reduction in intensity of any strong stimulus is reinforcing. Thus *any* stimulus may be a drive and a reinforcer—this role is not limited to "stimuli characteristic of a need." Miller's argument does not readily explain studies in which a stimulus increase is found to be reinforcing.

A common position concerning the nature of reinforcement is that no explanation is necessary. Thus Skinner (1938, 1948, 1953) says that any stimulus that increases the probability of response is a reinforcer by definition. He argues that this treatment is not circular. If a stimulus is identified as a reinforcer in one situation, it can then be used as a reinforcer in another situation, a condition that makes the definition general rather than circular. This position does not provide for an independent determination of the status of a stimulus as a reinforcer, and thus effectively eliminates the possibility of testing the question of whether reinforcement is necessary for learning. That proposition is accepted as a primitive axiom and is not to be questioned.

PUNISHMENT AND REINFORCEMENT

The role of punishment in learning is by no means simple, and the application of punishment to a response may have unpredictable and varied consequences. In fact, one of the basic unsolved problems in learning might be called the *punishment paradox*. The application of punishment to a response usually leads to its prompt disappearance. The reader should recall two studies discussed earlier. In one, Bower, Fowler, and Trapold (1959) demonstrated that the greater the amount of reduction in shock provided when the rat reached a goal box, the faster it ran. The results of this study are shown in Figure 4.7. In treating the effects of punishment of the response on extinction, the study by Seligman and Campbell (1965) was described in which shocking the animals for running to a goal box produced faster extinction with greater punishment for responding. These results fulfill what might be called the "normally" expected effects of punishment. However, there are situations in which the application of punishment leads to repetition of the response or even performance of the response in a manner suggesting that punishment has produced greater learning. Brown, Martin, and Morrow (1964) performed a study in which rats were trained to escape shock by running to a safe goal box. During extinction, the start box was safe for all, but some animals were shocked in part or all of the alley. In one experiment, animals shocked in the runway did not extinguish faster than animals that were not shocked, and in another experiment, animals that were shocked for making the response extinguished even more slowly. The authors refer to this performance as "masochistic-like" behavior.

A dramatic example of punishment leading to repetition of the response is any one of a set of experiments by Maier (1949) and his students. Typically, an animal is induced to jump from a small platform toward one of two windows which contain stimulus cards. Animals can be taught to discriminate between the two cards if jumping to the correct one leads to access to the platform and food behind the card and jumping to the incorrect one leads to a bump on the nose and a fall into a net several feet below. In one study by Ellen and Feldman (1958), for example, animals were induced to jump when the problem was unsolvable. Under these conditions, the animal falls into the net about half of the time whatever he chooses to do. After a few trials the animal is reluctant to jump, and some form of punishment is needed, such as shock on the platform to induce him to jump. Most animals will choose one side or the other and jump exclusively to that side. At this point, the problem is made solvable so that either a light or a dark card is consistently correct. Most animals persist in jumping to one side throughout a large number of trials. Maier (1949) calls this stereotyped, inappropriate behavior *fixated*. He calls the process by which it became fixated one of *frustration*. If small runways are provided on half of the trials so that fixated animals can walk to the cards instead of jumping, three distinct groups develop. One group quickly learns to walk to the correct card and soon learns to jump correctly. Another group remains fixated on both the jumping response and the walking response. A third group responds correctly when the runways are in place but continues to jump to one side whether the correct or the incorrect card appears in that window. In this case, it is clear that punishment has led to behavior which is abnormally resistant to extinction. Furthermore, since one group of animals responds appropriately to the positive stimulus when the runway is in place but does not when there is no runway, punishment has produced opposite effects in the same animal in very similar situations.

This small sample of research on the effects of punishment on behavior makes it clear that a major problem exists in specifying the conditions in which punishment eliminates a response as distinguished from those in which it leads to repetition or to abnormally inflexible behavior. Although there is no simple answer to this problem, some situations may be understood by determining what response is induced by the punishment itself. Thus Fowler and Miller (1963) trained rats to run down a runway to obtain food. In addition they arranged the situation so that some rats could be shocked on the forepaws and others shocked on the hindpaws during the performance of the running response. They found that shock on the forepaws produced slower running and shock on the hindpaws produced faster running. The greater the intensity of the shock, the greater they found the two effects to be. This study makes clear that one of the effects of punishment is to produce a response which may be either compatible or incompatible with the ongoing behavior. However, the variety of effects of punishment on behavior is sufficiently great that no simple solution to the punishment paradox emerges.

PROBLEMS IN THE NECESSARY CONDITIONS FOR LEARNING

While conditioning and instrumental-learning procedures will almost always produce learning, a number of questions arise concerning the necessity of fulfilling all of the conditions of these procedures. If some elements of them are omitted, does learning still occur? In the conditioning paradigm in which three elements are specified, the CS followed by the US followed by the UR, one can wonder whether the CS is necessary on every trial or whether association can occur between the two stimuli even though the response does not occur. Is the response necessary? In the selective learning paradigm, the three terms are the stimulus, the response, and the reinforcement. The question here is whether learning can occur in the absence of the response, the reinforcement, or both. Such questions are equally applicable to the extinction process. Let us turn to sensory preconditioning and some other approaches that attempt to answer questions pertaining to the necessary conditions for learning.

SENSORY PRECONDITIONING

If two neutral stimuli are paired together over a number of trials, and one of them is subsequently conditioned to a response, will the other elicit the response? The answer is that it will, and some form of association occurs when the neutral stimuli are paired together. A basic study which defines sensory preconditioning was done by Brogden (1939). He presented a buzz and a light simultaneously 200 times to eight dogs. He then conditioned a leg flexion response to one of the stimuli using shock as the US. In 20 test trials he used the stimulus that had not been conditioned to the response but which had been paired with the CS in sensory preconditioning. He obtained CRs on about half of the trials of the 20-trial test session. Dogs which had not had the sensory preconditioning of the two stimuli averaged about a half of a response in the test period.

While sensory preconditioning certainly does occur, and therefore it can be said that conditioning occurred in the absence of the occurrence of the response, other studies appear to show that associations formed in this way do not follow the simple principles of conditioning. Hoffeld, Kendall, Thompson, and Brogden (1960) varied the number of pairings of the two neutral stimuli in the sensory-conditioning phase to determine if a normal learning curve would arise. They used a six second tone and a two second light in preconditioning and gave 0, 1, 2, 4, 8, 10, 20, 40, 80, 200, 400, or 800 trials to 12 different groups of cats. Conditioning consisted of two seconds of light followed by .1 second of shock. In the test, the tone was presented alone. No simple learning curve appeared. The curve rose quickly to a maximum with four pairings of the two neutral stimuli and then fell to a relatively steady level. One could almost conclude that the sensory association gained its maximum strength in three or four pairings and did not increase significantly thereafter. This is in contrast to a normal acquisition curve in conditioning such as that in Figure 4.1.

Sensory preconditioning does not seem to produce a typical generalization gradient. Kendall and Thompson (1960) paired a tone of 250 cps with one of 2,000 cps in 20 trials of preconditioning with cats. Then the 250-cps tone was paired with shock. The cats were then tested for conditioning using tones of 500, 1,000, 2,000, 4,000 and 8,000 cps, thus one to five octaves above the CS. They found about the same number of responses to tones from 500 to 4,000 cps, and virtually none at 8,000 cps. Thus the generalization curve was essentially flat instead of sloping, and the authors conclude that sensory conditioning is essentially an all-or-nothing affair.

CS-CS interval in sensory conditioning does not seem to produce the same results as CS-US interval in normal conditioning. In four quite different studies by Silver and Meyer (1954), Coppock (1958), Hoffeld, Thompson, and Brogden (1958), and Wickens and Cross (1963) backward sensory conditioning proved to be nearly as effective as forward conditioning, and the best forward interval was not at about 500σ, as is true in classical conditioning. In fact, in the Hoffeld, Thompson, and Brogden study cited, it was generally true that the longer the interval the better the sensory conditioning in tests with intervals ranging from zero to four seconds.

OCCASIONAL OMISSION OF THE CS

In a human eyelid conditioning study, Kimble, Mann, and Dufort (1955) omitted the CS on the middle 20 trials of 60 trials of training, a form of pseudoconditioning procedure, and could find no difference between this group and one for which the CS had been present on all 60 trials. Dufort and Kimble (1958) could replicate the finding, but in studies by Goodrich, Ross, and Wagner (1957) and by McAllister and McAllister (1960), such omissions of the CS led to poorer performance. While the problem remains unresolved, it seems likely that the associative aspect (H or habit) and the motivational aspect (D or drive) may well develop somewhat differently in response to number or presentations.

LATENT LEARNING AND LATENT EXTINCTION

The name *latent learning* arose from an experimental problem in which an animal was permitted to explore an environment without receiving reward. He was subsequently provided with reward to determine if there was "latent" or unexpressed learning that had occurred during the nonrewarded experience. In other forms of the latent-learning experiment, animals are permitted to experience the location of a goal object, such as food, either when they are satiated for food and water or when they are strongly motivated and rewarded for another goal object. They demonstrate latent learning by later going to the food when they are hungry.

A fairly typical latent-learning study is that of Spence, Bergmann, and Lippitt (1950). They ran rats in a T maze while the rats were satiated for food and water; food was in one arm and water was in the other. The animals were induced to run by permitting them to return to the home or "social" cage after each run. After training, some of the animals were made hungry and some thirsty, and then they were tested for latent learning. On the following day, the drive states of the two groups were reversed and the animals tested again. On both days there was a tendency for the animals to choose the side appropriate to their drive state, indicating that they had learned something about the location of food and water during the period of nonreward.

A great many studies of latent learning have been carried out (see Kimble, 1961), with some affirming the existence of latent learning and others failing to find such evidence. In spite of the frequent negative results, the large number of studies showing positive results appears to justify the conclusion that some latent learning does occur in the absence of relevant reinforcement. However, latent-learning procedures usually prove to be inefficient compared to those involving direct reward to a motivated organism.

In studies of *latent extinction,* the usual procedure is to train an animal to make a response, permit him to experience the fact that the reward has been removed without his making the response, and then demonstrate the effect of this experience on his performance in extinction. The classic study of latent extinction is that of Seward and Levy (1949). They gave two groups of rats 10 training trials in which the rats ran over a narrow elevated runway from one platform to receive food on a second platform. One group was given latent-extinction experience by being placed on the goal platform from which the food was removed both before and between extinction trials. The other group spent equivalent periods on a neutral platform. The latent-extinction group showed significantly faster extinction than the control group. Thus it does not appear to be necessary for the *response* to be followed by nonreward for some degree of extinction to take place.

ACQUISITION AND EXTINCTION WITHOUT RESPONDING

The occurrence of a response can be prevented by temporary surgical intervention or through the use of drugs. The CS and US can then be paired any number of times while the animal is unable to perform the response. After recovery from the surgery or after the drug effects have worn off, the animal can be tested to see if learning occurred when it was unable to respond. Similarly, an animal may be conditioned and the response prevented from occurring during extinction while the CS is presented a number of times. After recovery, performance should reveal the effectiveness of such an extinction procedure.

A typical study of learning without responding is that of Lauer (1951). He inserted an electrode into the motor nerve of a hind leg of a dog. The animal was then given a type of curare that acts to prevent muscular response. While the dog was curarized, a tone was paired a number of times with shock to the leg that could ordinarily have produced a flexion response. After the dog had recovered from the effects of the curare, tests revealed that some learning had occurred during training even though the response had been prevented during the acquisition trials. Similar results were obtained by Kellogg, Scott, Davis, and Wolf (1940) when the response was prevented during training by crushing the motor roots of spinal nerves. When the motor fibers had regenerated, the animals showed evidence of having been conditioned. Beck and Doty (1957) confirmed these findings while using several surgical and drug procedures to prevent the response during training in cats.

Black (1958) used a curare to prevent the occurrence of an avoidance response in dogs during extinction. His general procedure was to train dogs to turn their heads and push a panel to avoid shock. When the response was well established, some animals were given 55 extinction trials while they were curarized and others were given the same number of trials while free to make the response. In 400 additional extinction trials during which all animals were free to respond to the CS, the animals with the 55 extinction trials under curare showed evidence of much faster extinction than the control animals. A variety of interpretations of this result are possible. It could be argued that making the response itself has secondary reinforcing properties which ordinarily extend the extinction process by providing some reinforcement during extinction. The 55 trials during which the response was prevented could not provide this hypothesized source of reinforcement. On the other hand, the avoidance procedure is one in which successful avoidance prevents the occurrence of the UCs. In normal extinction, the animal has no means of discovering that the shock is no longer present as long as he continues to make the responses. The 55 trials under curare provided this information to the experimental animals.

These studies seem to indicate that both conditioning and extinction can occur when the response is physically prevented from occurring. Thus association between stimuli can occur on the basis of stimulus properties other than their capacity to produce the revelant observable unconditioned response.

THE THEORETICAL ISSUES

The basic theoretical issues involved in studies of the necessary conditions for learning are frequently reduced to two. One issue is whether association takes place between the stimuli involved, a position referred to as S-S learning, or whether learning always involves an association between stimuli and responses, S-R learning. The second issue is whether simple *contiguity* is a sufficient principle for learning or whether some form of *reinforcement* is necessary. Probably the most reasonable conclusion is that neither issue involves simple alternatives: therefore, both S-S and S-R learning occur, as do learning through contiguity and learning through reinforcement.

LEARNING TO LEARN

Does the rate of learning improve as an organism learns successive problems? The answer to the general question is clearly affirmative, although there are a number of issues that arise in experiments designed to establish the truth of this proposition.

The simplest test of this question can be made by training an animal to make a response through reinforcement, instituting extinction when the learning criterion is met, reestablishing reinforcement when the response is extinguished, and repeating the process. The question is whether acquisition and extinction occur more rapidly as the process continues. In this respect, the acquisition phase appears to be different from the extinction phase. Lauer and Estes (1955) trained animals to jump from a platform to one of two windows to obtain a food reward. The choice of either window was rewarded, and learning was measured in terms of speed of response (1/latency). There were four periods of reinforcement separated by three periods of nonreinforcement. In successive reinforcement periods, the rate of learning was faster, and the speed of jumping at the end was faster. However, the results in extinction were different. During successive periods of nonreinforcement the animals slowed down a lesser amount and at a slower rate. Thus they extinguished more slowly and showed less extinction.

The difference in effect of repeated learning and repeated extinction on the acquisition phase as opposed to the extinction phase is even more pronounced in a study by Lauer and Carterette (1957). Two groups of animals had two trials a day for 54 days. One group was reinforced on all trials, while the other had nine days of reinforcement followed by six days of nonreinforcement, with four reinforcement periods separated by three nonreinforcement periods. Furthermore, since a straight runway was used in this study, two scores, starting speed and running speed, were obtained. After the first acquisition phase, the group with interspersed periods of extinction showed faster starting speeds and somewhat faster running times during reinforcement than the group that was continuously reinforced. Thus, periods of extinction actually produced higher performance levels than were produced by continued reinforcement. The difference between acquisition and extinction was even more marked with respect to starting speed. During the first extinction period, the starting speed became slower than it was for the animals under continued reinforcement. During the second extinction period there was little difference between the two groups, and during the third extinction period, the group for which reinforcement had been removed actually started faster than the group under continued reinforcement. Thus, with repeated reinforcement periods followed by periods of nonreinforcement, animals seem to learn faster each time, but extinguish more slowly, if they can be said to extinguish at all.

However, it seems likely that if training were extended over a great many periods of acquisition and extinction, a stage would be reached in which both faster learning and faster extinction occurred. It will be recalled that a small amount of overlearning on a difficult problem produced an increase in resistance to extinction in a study by Mackintosh

(1963), while large amounts of overlearning produced progressively faster extinction in a simple problem, in a study by Ison (1962) shown in Figure 4.17.

However, the effect of such alternation may be very different in avoidance learning, as shown in a study by Jacobs (1963). He trained rats to choose one of two compartments to avoid shock. He opened a starting-compartment door, and after 15 seconds (7.5 seconds for another group) turned on a shock which remained on until the animal reached the correct goal compartment. When this response was learned, shock was omitted and the response extinguished to a criterion of eight successive trials with a latency longer than 15 seconds. In this study, there were six periods of acquisition followed by six periods of extinction. Acquisition improved between the first and second acquisition periods, but showed no further demonstrable improvement. However, successive extinctions required increasingly greater numbers of trials, as may be seen in Figure 4.20. Thus successive periods of acquisition and extinction appear to lead to faster learning and slower extinction.

There have been a number of studies of repeated reversals in discrimination problems. In one of the classic studies, North (1950) trained animals to make one of two responses to achieve a food reward. Then the problem was reversed by rewarding the other response. In reversal learning, one can think of the reversal task as being one in which the first response must be unlearned for the second to be learned, thus combining both acquisition and extinction. North carried his animals through 12 successive reversals using a number of different procedures. The results in Figure 4.21 show that the first reversal, produced more errors than original learning, but after the third reversal, the animals made fewer errors and the curve seems to be dropping throughout its course. While there have been a number of studies in which improvement has failed to appear with successive reversals, others such as those of Birch, Ison, and Sperling (1960), Mackintosh (1963), and Stretch, McGonigle, and Rodger (1963) found results very similar to those of North. Under most circumstances, then, one can expect at first poorer and then progressively better performance with successive reversals. This means, of course, that after a few reversals, extinction of the old response cannot grow progressively longer as was found in the case of successive acquisition and extinction periods.

After the first reversal, the animal is relearning a problem that was learned before. One might ask whether the learning to learn shown in Figure 4.21 is a general improvement which would be demonstrated on all problems or whether the improvement is confined to the particular learning situation. Mackintosh (1962) made a comparison between reversal learning and learning a new problem. He also explored the effect of the amount of overlearning of the original problem on both

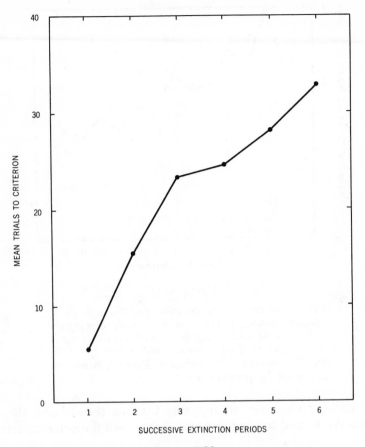

Figure 4.20

The progressive increase in the number of trials required to reach the criterion of extinction in successive periods of extinction of an avoidance response following periods of acquisition. (Adapted from Jacobs, 1963. Copyright 1963 by The American Psychological Association and reproduced by permission.)

reversal learning and learning a new problem. To do this, he first trained 24 rats to choose between a black stimulus and a white stimulus in a jumping-stand situation. The animals required about 75–76 trials. A third of the animals were given 75 extra overtraining trials, and another third were given 150 extra overtraining trials. Each of the three groups were then divided in half, with four animals trained to reverse the original black-white discrimination and the other four trained to choose between horizontal and vertical stripes. The data in Table 4.3 show that the effect

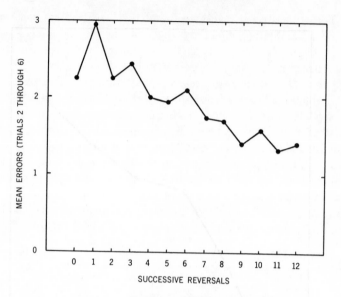

Figure 4.21

Change in error score on trials two through six of original learning and successive reversals showing the improvement in learning score with repeated experience. (Adapted from North, 1950. Copyright 1950 by The American Psychological Association and reproduced by permission.)

of overlearning was quite the opposite between reversal and the new problem. As original training was extended beyond the criterion, reversal

Table 4.3

Effects of overlearning on subsequent reversal learning and learning a new discrimination problem (Mackintosh, 1963).

TRAINING CONDITIONS ON ORIGINAL PROBLEM	TRIALS TO REACH CRITERION	
	REVERSAL LEARNING	LEARNING NEW PROBLEM
Trained to criterion	124.75	84.25
Trained 75 trials beyond criterion	89.50	105.00
Trained 150 trials beyond criterion	78.25	140.00

learning became easier and easier, but the effect of overtraining was to make the learning of the new problem more and more difficult. The terms usually used to refer to these effects are *positive* and *negative* transfer. Thus the effect of overlearning of the first problem was positive transfer, or a facilitative effect on the learning of the reverse of the original problem. However, overlearning had a negative transfer, or inhibiting effect, on the learning of a new one.

That the negative-transfer effect is a temporary one in a longer series of problems is made clear in the work of Harlow (1949, 1959) on *learning sets*. He and Margaret (Kuenne) Harlow have demonstrated repeatedly that both monkeys and young children show progressive improvement in learning new problems. For example, monkeys can be trained to choose one of two objects on the basis of any one of a number of differences between the two, such as shape or color. The first learning period might require several hundred trials. However, if an animal learns many such problems, it will learn to learn, and become very efficient in solving new problems in a very small number of trials. Figure 4.22 shows

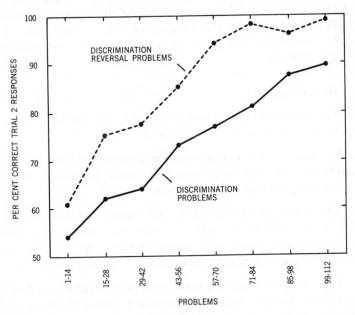

Figure 4.22

Discrimination and discrimination-reversal curves based on the percent of correct second-trial responses showing the development of learning sets through a long series of problems. (Adapted from Harlow, 1949. Copyright 1949 by The American Psychological Association and reproduced by permission.)

the progress of a group of eight monkeys learning a series of discrimination problems and subsequent progress of the same group in learning a series of discrimination reversal problems. In both cases, the curves are approaching 100 percent. Since the first trial of a new problem or a reversal is an "information" trial, 100 percent performance on the second trial would represent maximum efficiency of learning in a single trial. It should be noted, however, that the demonstration of learning sets involves a skill within a narrow range of similar problems. The animals had reached the 90 percent point in solving discrimination problems but dropped to slightly over 60 percent in the first block of discrimination reversal problems. They again exceeded the 90 percent level only after solving more than 50 of the discrimination reversal problems.

Acquiring a "set" to learn in a certain type of situation is not confined to higher organisms such as monkeys and children. Wright, Kay, and Sime (1963) have succeeded in demonstrating the development of learning sets in rats. They trained 16 rats to discriminate shapes in a series of problems. This is a difficult discrimination problem for rats, but all learned some of the problems, and three of the animals succeeded in solving 32 problems over a seven month period. Animals that solved an appreciable number of the problems showed progressive improvement in learning efficiency.

Let us summarize:

1. It appears that overlearning produces first an increase in resistance to extinction and then a decrease as training is extended.

2. In avoidance learning, alternation of periods of reinforcement and nonreinforcement results in progressively faster acquisition and indefinitely increasing resistance to extinction.

3. Alternation of periods of reinforcement and nonreinforcement probably leads to faster learning in successive periods. Resistance to extinction, however, tends to increase in successive periods but may decrease if the number of extinction periods is great enough.

4. Successive reversals of a two-choice problem produces first slower and then faster learning on each successive reversal, requiring that rate of extinction must increase and then decrease over a long series of reversals.

5. Overlearning of one problem slows up learning of a new problem in a short series of problems; in a long series of similar problems, learning sets develop which produce very rapid and highly efficient problem solutions.

While learning sets appear to be partly specific to the type of problem in which they are developed, the progress from alternation of periods of reinforcement and extinction, through reversal learning of the same problem, through the learning to learn a class of problems, suggests that something more than the single measured response is learned in a period of training. However it is characterized or explained, some positive transfer appears to occur and something like *learning to learn* is acquired.

OPERANT CONDITIONING
5

Operant conditioning is the name applied by Skinner (1938) to a procedure of exerting control over the behavior of an organism in a relatively free environment by means of the judicious application of reinforcement. In some of its applications, operant conditioning represents a maximum of flexibility—in contrast to the less flexible behavior involved in classical conditioning and in instrumental learning.

In classical conditioning, for example, one always starts with a response which is reliably elicited by a specific stimulus that is under the control of the experimenter. Thus by applying the stimulus, the experimenter can produce the response at will. The CS, the US, and the responses are all under the immediate and precise control of the experimenter. The flexibility in the situation is confined almost exclusively to the transfer of associative connection from the US to the CS. Skinner (1938) referred to this kind of learning situation as *respondent conditioning* to distinguish both the procedure and the process from the more flexible *operant conditioning*.

In instrumental learning, the behavior of the organism is almost always constrained in two ways. In most cases, the animal or person is placed in a situation in which the freedom to respond is limited by the apparatus or the situation to a small number of clearly specified alternatives. Sometimes this restriction is so severe that the organism is free only to sit or run down a runway. Rarely are the alternatives more than two or three. The second important constraint is that the learning process is almost always studied in terms of "trials" arranged by the experimenter. That is, the animal is placed in a situation by the experimenter, is permitted to choose one of the alternatives, is reinforced or not depending on the choice, and terminates the trial by his response. The process is then repeated in a number of discrete trials. This constraining procedure is referred to as being "experimenter-controlled."

Operant conditioning, on the other hand, is often referred to as being "subject-controlled." Typically the organism is free to do what it likes and when it likes. The experimenter exerts control over the behavior through the application of reinforcement. Thus the behavior is *emitted* by the organism in operant conditioning, rather than *elicited* through the application of an unconditioned stimulus as in respondent conditioning. Instead of "trials" in which the beginning is determined by the experimenter and the ending determined by the organism, in operant conditioning the organism determines the time of both the beginning and the end of the trial.

THE EXPERIMENTAL ANALYSIS OF BEHAVIOR

Operant conditioning is defined in terms of procedure. The program of research which grew out of it, however, has a number of special characteristics which do not necessarily follow from the procedure. Rather, they are important positions initiated by Skinner (1938, 1953, 1951, 1961) and developed, in part, by numerous others on fundamental issues relevant to the field of learning and learning theory. The whole complex of specialized terminology, style of experimentation, and attitudes toward theoretical and experimental issues, as well as directions of major research, has come to be referred to as aspects of *the experimental analysis of behavior*. A few of these characteristics and problems need further discussion.

REINFORCEMENT

Skinner does not ask why a stimulus is reinforcing, he only seeks to determine that a stimulus has reinforcing properties. He feels that such properties can be shown by a simple test: Choose some discrete aspect of the behavior emitted by an organism—one that occurs often enough to be counted. Count the frequency over a fixed period of time so that you determine the rate of emission of that bit of behavior. (That *rate* of emission is called the *operant level*.) Then, for a period, follow each instance of an emission of that bit of behavior by a stimulus. If the rate of emission increases, then you have established the reinforcing properties of the stimulus. Skinner argues that this defining procedure is not circular because once it is determined that a stimulus does have reinforcing properties, it can then be used as a reinforcer in many situations. Thus, the "transsituational" property of reinforcers is said to establish their generality.

In Skinner's terms, reinforcing stimuli may be either positive or negative. A *positive* reinforcing stimulus increases the rate of operant responding when it is *applied* immediately after each response. A *negative* reinforcer increases the probability of a response when it is *removed* immediately after each response. Punishment is defined as the removal of a positive reinforcer or the application of a negative reinforcing stimulus.

THEORY

Skinner's refusal to ask why a stimulus has reinforcing properties is part of his general resistance to the formulation of theoretical propositions. He takes the position that when we know enough to exercise *control* over behavior, we shall have no need for theory. Skinner's theorizing about behavior thus remains consistently informal, inductive, and implicit rather than formal, deductive, and explicit. He prefers to develop broad empirical generalizations rather than specific constructs. In the terms of theory structure as diagramed elsewhere in this volume and in *Psychology as a Natural and Social Science* (Walker, 1967), Skinner's theory has no intervening variables, and an attempt to diagram it would produce an empty box.

EXPERIMENTAL STYLE

In *Basic Statistics*, Hays (1967) explains several ways to determine the statistical significance of an experimental finding. Most procedures involve dividing the difference between the mean scores of two groups by an estimate of the variability in score within the groups. If the resulting ratio is as large as a predetermined standard, the result is said to be statistically significant. There are generally two ways to increase the size of the ratio. Since the estimate of variability is determined by N (the number of organisms) and by the variability of the behavior in question, one can choose to increase the size of N or to decrease the variability. Increasing the size of N is straightforward and laborious. Producing a decrease in variability means increasing the quality of the experimenter's control so that factors other than the one under study cannot produce unsystematic variation in the scores. Skinner clearly chooses the latter procedure and undertakes to exert sufficient control over the behavior in question to make a statistical test unnecessary. Thus he chooses to exercise experimental rather than statistical control over his subjects. It should be obvious that this choice leads to an ultimate style of research in which a single organism is a sufficient "group" for the establishment of a principle. Additional organisms are then tested only to determine that the principle works with all or most individuals.

CUMULATIVE CURVES

Data about an individual performance can be recorded by a cumulative recorder, which consists of a pen that draws a line on a roll of paper moving at a constant rate. Each time the animal makes a response, the pen moves a fixed, small distance across the roll of paper. If the animal responds rapidly, the pen will describe a steep slope across the paper. If the animal responds slowly, the slope will be less steep. If the animal is irregular in his rate of responding, the curve will have a variable slope.

Figure 5.1 is a curve that might have resulted from the following simple demonstration. Suppose we place a hungry animal in a Skinner box and leave him there for a while. A Skinner box is a device that is usually barren except for a small lever and food tray. It is likely that

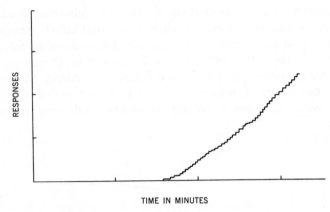

TIME IN MINUTES

Figure 5.1

Drawing representing a cumulative record of the acquisition of an operant response. (In this aspect, the paper moved from right to left; on a cumulative recorder, the paper would have unrolled upward.)

sooner or later he will accidentally press the lever while exploring the box, and a pellet of food will be delivered to the food tray. Pressing the lever will cause the pen to trace a notch across the moving roll of paper. The pen will then draw a straight line until the lever is pressed again. If the animal presses steadily, the pen will trace a series of notches across the moving paper. [Although Figure 5.1 happens to be an artist's drawing, one of the virtues of cumulative records is that they can be photographed directly, for there is no need to "process" such data.]

The curve in Figure 5.1 rises almost abruptly from the baseline, and its characteristic slope is established almost immediately. It is obvious that once the animal pressed the lever, little time was spent in learning to associate the pressing of the lever with the delivery of food. Thus, there was very little "learning" in the sense of learning how to do something. Had there been appreciable learning in this sense, the curve would have risen slowly, with an increasing slope, until full learning was complete, after which the slope would have remained constant.

The interpretation of Figure 5.1 points up an essential difference between operant conditioning and other forms of "learning." If one makes a distinction between learning and performance, operant conditioning is largely concerned with factors which influence the performance level rather than factors which influence learning. Learning is reflected in the rate of approach to the asymptote of a learning curve. In terms of a cumulative record, operant conditioning is largely concerned with factors which will influence the asymptote of a learning curve—not the rate of approach to it.

To continue our demonstration, if we stop delivering food when the animal presses the lever, we shall have established experimental extinction conditions. Figure 5.2 is the kind of record we might expect. The slope of the curve indicates rapid responding at the outset of experimental extinction. This burst is followed by a pause. As extinction continues, the bursts of responding become shorter and pauses longer until the curve becomes essentially horizontal, indicating no further responses.

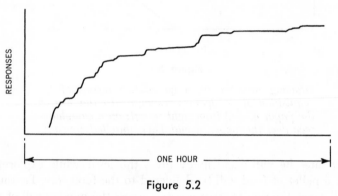

Figure 5.2

Drawing representing a cumulative record of the experimental extinction of an operant response.

Figure 5.2 illustrates another characteristic of operant conditioning. Instead of placing exclusive emphasis on extracting data and calculating various values, one can "interpret the grain" of a cumulative record. The bursts and pauses of Figure 5.2, the scallops of Figure 5.3, and the bursts and pauses in Figure 5.8 are characteristic of the "grain of the record." A variety of explanations have been offered to explain scallops, bursts, and pauses.

SCHEDULES OF REINFORCEMENT

The capacity to delay gratification is regarded as a sign of maturity in humans. A similar capacity is often seen in animals—a dog will wait a long while and will do a great many things for an occasional pat on the head. A major experimental innovation of Skinner's (1938) is the deliberate omission of reinforcement after some of the responses emitted by an organism. This procedure, in contrast to *continuous* reinforcement, is referred to as *intermittent* or partial reinforcement. Partial reinforcement has been applied in a great many patterns, called *schedules* of reinforcement.

RATIO REINFORCEMENT

If reinforcement is offered only after an animal has made a fixed number of responses, say five, then he is on a *fixed-ratio* schedule. In training an animal or human to perform on a fixed-ratio schedule, especially if a small ratio is used, one must generally start with continuous reinforcement until the organism is responding well. Then intermittent reinforcement can be instituted and only gradually can small ratios be imposed. Three curves that are typical of performances under fixed-ratio schedules may be seen in Figure 5.3. The curves represent the behavior

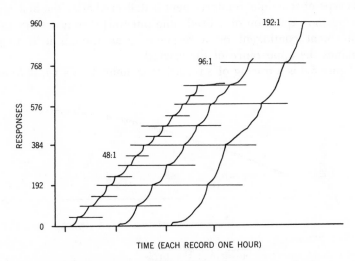

TIME (EACH RECORD ONE HOUR)

Figure 5.3

Performance curves of three animals under fixed-ratio reinforcement schedules. Reinforcements are marked by horizontal lines. The ratios are indicated by the numbers. (Figure 91 from The Behavior of Organisms *by B. F. Skinner. Copyright 1938 by Appleton-Century-Crofts, Inc. Reprinted by permission of Appleton-Century-Crofts.)*

of animals that were induced to work on fixed-ratio schedules of 48:1, 96:1, or 192:1. After each reinforcement (indicated by a horizontal line), the animals paused, then responded at a positively accelerating rate—the most rapid rate of responding was just before the next reinforcement. Ratios much higher than those shown in Figure 5.3 have been found effective. While there are limits to this process, it is astonishing how hard an organism can be induced to work to receive a single reinforcement.

Ratio schedules can be made variable rather than fixed. If an organism is reinforced once in five responses on the average, he is said to be on a *variable-ratio* schedule. Performances of animals on variable-ratio schedules tend to be somewhat higher in rate than performances obtained on equivalent fixed-ratio schedules. Their performance curves fail to show such pronounced "scallops" as those evident in the grain of the curves in Figure 5.3. Since an animal does not know precisely when to expect reinforcement, his tendency to speed up in anticipation is not so pronounced.

INTERVAL REINFORCEMENT

Another type of schedule involves reinforcement at a *fixed interval*. In this type of schedule, reinforcement is delivered after the first response following the expiration of a fixed time interval. It is necessary to make reinforcement contingent on a response, even though it is time that determines the appearance of the reward.

Figure 5.4 is a tracing of a record of an animal on a *variable-interval*

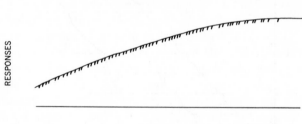

TIME

Figure 5.4

Performance of an animal under a one minute variable-interval schedule of reinforcement by water after water deprivation. Each mark on the curve represents a reinforcement. (Redrawn from Figure 11 of The Experimental Analysis of Behavior *by Thom Verhave. Copyright © 1966 by Meredith Publishing Company. Reprinted by permission of Appleton-Century-Crofts.)*

schedule. This record, taken from Verhave (1966) represents the performance of a rat pressing a lever to receive water on a variable-interval schedule of one minute. The animal had been without water for 22 hours. His rate of responding, as revealed by the slope of the curve, remained fairly constant over a considerable period and then gradually became negatively accelerated as the animal approached satiation for water. The curve in Figure 5.4 is typical of interval-schedule performances.

Other Schedules. While the simple ratio and interval schedules are the most commonly employed, a large number of others have been used. They have such names as tandem, mixed, interlocking, alternative, concurrent, conjunctive, interpolated, adjusting, and differential-rate schedules. As the names imply, some are complicated, and some involve simultaneous use of more than one reinforcement pattern. Possibly, the most productive schedule is the one that rewards only rapid responding. For descriptions of these and other schedules of reinforcement, the reader should consult Ferster and Skinner (1957) or Verhave (1966).

RESISTANCE TO EXTINCTION

One of the more interesting findings that has emerged from the study of operant conditioning is the high resistance to extinction which follows removal of all reward after intermittent reinforcement. An organism will respond far longer in the absence of reward after intermittent reinforcement than after continuous reinforcement.

Figure 5.5 is an illustration of the higher resistance to extinction with intermittent reinforcement. In this case, the measure of performance is running speed in a short runway. These results are from a study by Weinstock (1954). He trained four groups of 12 rats each to run down a short runway to food while hungry. They had one trial a day for 70 days during which the four groups were reinforced on 30 percent, 50 percent, 80 percent, or 100 percent of the trials. Then, during a period of extinction, none of the rats was reinforced for 20 days. Weinstock found no difference in running speed between the four groups during training, but there are fairly clear differences during extinction as illustrated in Figure 5.5. Although curves do not maintain a simple order throughout the trials, there is a clear tendency for intermittently reinforced animals to run faster than continuously reinforced animals. Furthermore, in terms of persistence, there is a clear tendency for the groups to differ during the last 12 days in such a way that the smaller their percentage of reinforcement was during the training, the faster they continued to run during the latter part of the period of extinction.

The same phenomenon has been demonstrated in the slot-machine-playing behavior of human subjects in three studies by Lewis and Duncan (1956, 1957, 1958). The three studies were sufficiently similar that the results from all three have been plotted in Figure 5.6. In each case, subjects were asked to play a slot-machine-like device and given an

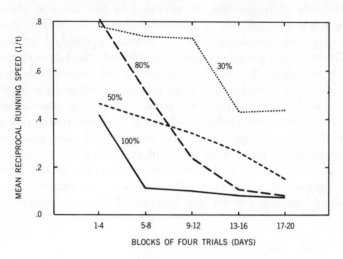

Figure 5.5

Experimental extinction of running speed in rats in runway resulting from different percentages of partial reinforcement during training. (Adapted from Weinstock, 1954. Copyright 1954 by The American Psychological Association and reproduced by permission.)

unlimited (for all practical purposes) supply of disks to be used in playing. They were told that they could play as long as they liked and that they would receive a dime for each disk they received as a payoff from the machine. In all cases, there was a brief period during which the device paid off by some percentage of reinforcements for each group, ranging from zero percent to 100 percent. Then the device ceased to pay. The relevant measure of performance was the number of times the subjects then pulled the lever without further reinforcement. Because there was great variability in the scores achieved by the different subjects within each group, the scores were converted to logarithms and the means of the logarithmic values were plotted. Figure 5.6 shows clearly that the smaller the percentage of intermittent reinforcement during the training period, the longer the subjects persisted in pulling the handle after no further disks were forthcoming from the machine.

It should be noted that none of these studies comparing the effect of different percentage of reinforcement on number of responses to extinction involved the use of cumulative recorders and the presentation of unprocessed records. In the Lewis and Duncan studies and the study by Weinstock, traditional methods were used to record the data, and the results reported are in terms of group performances.

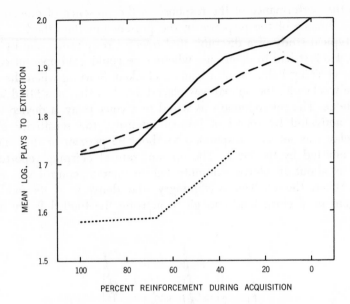

Figure 5.6

Number of responses during experimental extinction of a lever-pulling response in human subjects resulting from differences in percentages of reinforcement during training. (Adapted from Lewis and Duncan, 1956, Lewis and Duncan, 1957, and Lewis and Duncan, 1958. Copyright 1956, 1957, 1958 by The American Psychological Association and reproduced by permission.)

The studies discussed are a sample of a very large group of studies of the effects of intermittent reinforcement on resistance to extinction. An old but comprehensive review of partial reinforcement, including efforts to give explanations of the effect, is contained in Jenkins and Stanley (1950). Several textbooks and monographs also contain summary discussions. See Ferster and Skinner (1957), Keller and Schoenfeld (1950), Kimble (1961), and Skinner (1938, 1953, and 1961).

DISCRIMINATION

Discrimination learning in operant conditioning follows a pattern similar to discrimination learning in other forms of training. The basic procedure is to present one stimulus in the presence of which the operant response will be reinforced and another stimulus in the presence of which the response will not be reinforced. Evidence of discrimination will be the performance of the response in the presence of one stimulus and the absence of the response in the presence of the other.

A typical study of a discriminated operant response is one by Lane (1960). He first had to determine whether he could gain operant control over the chirping behavior of a bantam chicken. Starting when the chick was five weeks old, the animal was placed in a box that was fitted with a microphone. The microphone was wired to a voice relay, a device which can be activated by sound of critical intensity; the sensitivity of the voice relay was set so it responded to about 95 percent of the chirping sounds emitted by the chick. The operant rate of chirping reported by Lane was about 16 chirps a minute before operant control was established. When the chicken was hungry, the delivery of its food was contingent on a chirp loud enough to activate the food delivery mech-

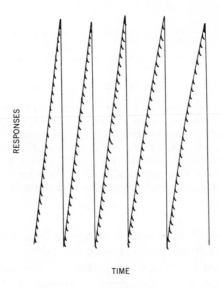

RESPONSES

TIME

Figure 5.7

Cumulative response curve for the chirp response of one chicken under a fixed-ratio schedule of reinforcement. The chick was reinforced for every twentieth chirp; reinforcements are represented by the marks on the rising line. The period represented is slightly more than 16.5 minutes, with approximately 2,800 responses during the period. There are approximately 140 reinforcements on the record with animals receiving a reinforcement about once every seven seconds. (From Lane, 1960. Copyright 1960 by The American Association for the Advancement of Science. Reprinted by permission of the author and publisher.)

anism. When the mechanism was activated, a food tray was made available to the chicken for a period of four seconds.

Operant control was established, and a fixed-ratio schedule was instituted so that the food tray was presented for a four second period only after every twentieth chirp. Under these conditions, the rate of chirping increased sharply. Figure 5.7 is a drawing representing the cumulative record of the chirping behavior of a chicken after chirping in the presence of the fixed ratio of reinforment was well established. The rate of responding in Figure 5.7 is fairly high and uniform, with reinforcements being achieved about every seven seconds.

The operant level of chirping was about 24 chirps a minute before control was established, and the level was about 27 a minute when food was continuously present but not contingent upon chirping. Under a fixed ratio of reinforcement, the rate was approximately 115 a minute, somewhat slower on the average than the rate depicted in Figure 5.7.

To establish that the high rate of chirping for food reinforcement represented real operant control, Lane established two control groups.

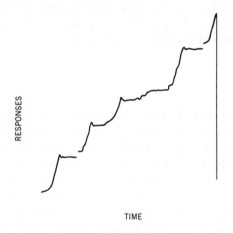

RESPONSES

TIME

Figure 5.8

Cumulative response curve for the chirp response of one chicken under a discriminative procedure. The curve represents approximately 450 responses made over a period of approximately 16.5 minutes. The rising portions are responses made in the presence of the positive, red light; reinforcement is represented by the four abrupt rises and drops in the curve. The flat portions indicate the low-response rate in the presence of the green, negative stimulus. (From Lane, 1960. Copyright 1960 by the American Association for the Advancement of Science. Reprinted by permission of the author and publisher.)

To one group, he delivered food at the same rate the animal had achieved under ratio reinforcement but made delivery of food independent of the chirping behavior. The rate of chirping was only nine a minute in this group. For another group, he made the appearance of the empty tray contingent upon chirping. Their rate was only eight a minute. Thus, simple stimulus change as represented by the appearance of the tray was not reinforcing.

In order to establish discrimination, Lane put the animal on a fixed-interval schedule while a red light was on. The animal was reinforced for the first chirp after two minutes had elapsed. Following one reinforcement on this fixed-interval schedule, a green light came on, and reinforcement became contingent on two minutes of silence. The red light and the green light were alternated. Figure 5.8 is drawn from a record made after discrimination was well established. It shows a pause after each reinforcement, then a positively accelerating rate of response, then the delivery of reinforcement; flat portions of the line indicate a lack of responses while the green light was on.

The animals learned this discrimination fairly well in about one hour. During the fourth hour of discrimination training, the average response rate in the presence of the positive red stimulus was about 22 a minute, and in the presence of the negative green stimulus about three a minute.

SHAPING

An important new principle of learning arises in the context of operant conditioning. That principle is the *shaping* of a response. In classical conditioning the US elicits a given response that is then associated with the CS. The CR is essentially the same as the UR. In instrumental learning, a limited number of discrete and completely identifiable responses can occur in the experimental situation because of the character of the apparatus. Operant conditioning offers the possibility of the development of an entirely new response in the situation—a response that would not occur naturally. Shaping is a highly descriptive name for the process. Starting with the responses the organism can and will make in a free environment, its behavior can be shaped into almost any pattern that is within the scope of the experimenter's or trainer's ingenuity.

EXTERNAL SHAPING

There are two ways to shape a response. The first way might be referred to as *external shaping*. If one wishes an organism to make a particular response—pressing a lever to obtain food, for example—the environment can be arranged to make this response more likely. If the space in which the animal is placed is large, he is likely to spend much more time exploring than if it is small. If the environment is complex, he will spend more time exploring than if it is simple. Therefore, choosing an enclosure that is small and simple should make the level-pressing response likely to occur sooner than choosing a space that is large and complex. If the lever is of such a size, shape, and in such a location that the animal is likely to press it accidentally, we can say that the response has been shaped by external means. In the language of Skinner, classically conditioned responses are rigidly shaped, while instrumental responses are somewhat less rigidly shaped but are still highly controlled externally.

INTERNAL SHAPING

The second kind of shaping—*internal shaping*—can occur in a very free, highly unstructured environment. It can be referred to as internal shaping because the constant strain imposed upon the behavior of the organism eventually lies within the organism rather than in the physical environment. Skinner (1951) describes the process in detail. As is evident in Skinner's account, the process of internal shaping can be described with considerable objectivity, but the execution of the process requires intelligence, ingenuity, and great skill on the part of the person doing the shaping.

Suppose we train a dog to dance on command. The first step described by Skinner (1951) is to establish some stimulus as a secondary reinforcer under the immediate and precise control of the experimenter. There are at least two reasons for this step. Shaping proceeds most rapidly and effectively when a reinforcement precisely coincides with the response. Most primary reinforcers, such as food for a hungry animal, require some time for delivery and consumption. Furthermore, a secondary reinforcer can be used many times without producing satiation, as would food, for instance. Thus, training can be extended much longer with a secondary reinforcer than with a food reward.

Any neutral stimulus could be used as a secondary reinforcing stimulus, but Skinner advises the use of a sound that does not require a preparatory move. Visual stimuli might not be seen by the dog, and a whistle requires an intake of breath that creates a delay in the sequence of response and reinforcement. Skinner, in his demonstration, used a "cricket" of the kind that children used to be able to buy or which used to come, occasionally, in a box of Cracker Jack. If no cricket is available, snapping one's fingers will do as well. The trainer should be sure the animal is quite hungry and should have an attractive food in pieces that are large enough for the animal to appreciate, but small enough so that a number can be used without satiating the animal. The fingers must be snapped as a piece of food is tossed to the animal; the sound should come immediately before the delivery of the food. In order to establish the snap of the fingers as a secondary reinforcer, some shaping of the behavior may be required. If the dog "begs" or tries to jump up on and paw the trainer, no reinforcement should be given. The snap and the food should be given only when the dog goes to the place where the trainer has decided that reinforcement will occur. Shortly, often within a minute, the trainer will be able to omit the food occasionally. The snap will have become a sufficiently strong reinforcer that it can be used alone. (During further training, it may occasionally be necessary to pair the snap with food to prevent complete experimental extinction of its secondary reinforcing property, but most of the training can be pursued with the snap as the only reward.)

One will then be able to begin shaping the dog's behavior into a pattern that resembles dancing. The method is often referred to as that of *successive approximation*. Suppose we decide that one dance step shall consist of shifting the dog's weight back and forth from one forepaw to the other. By watching the dog's feet, we can snap our fingers whenever we see the dog lift a paw. As soon as paw lifting occurs promptly, we can change to reinforcing only alternation between paws. Once that is established, we might choose to reward only a double shift. Finally we might reinforce only rhythmic changes in weight. We will have shaped a response that would not normally occur. Suppose we decide to train the dog to shift weight three times and then whirl around once. This could be accomplished by snapping our fingers only after the third weight shift until this dance step is occurring in triplets. Then we could begin to reinforce only those triplets that are followed by a tendency to turn to one side. Gradually we would be able to shape the turning into a full circle. We then would have *chained* the weight-shifting response to the turning response. By clever use of the method of successive approximation, and by chaining one response pattern to another, complex and highly unusual response patterns can be shaped. Limits on the complexity of the behavior that can be shaped are much more likely to be set by the limits and skill of the trainer than by the limited capacities for learning on the part of the animal being trained.

"SUPERSTITION"

To say that reinforcement is contingent upon a given pattern of behavior is only to say that the behavior was followed by reinforcement. The contingency may involve a casual relation between the response and the reinforcement. A steer put to graze in an old orchard may learn to shake the trees to obtain apples after an accidental bump or two against the trunk is followed by a shower of apples. In such a case, the behavior appears rational or even insightful. Reinforcement contingencies may be mediated by another organism, as is the case in which a trainer shaped the behavior. In that case the behavior may appear irrational and "superstitious" as long as we are not aware of the role of the trainer.

It is possible for complex patterns of behavior to be shaped and chained by an accidental contingency between the behavior and the reinforcement. Skinner (1948) has reported one demonstration of this kind of accidental chaining of complex behavior. He placed hungry pigeons in a box supplied with a food hopper. In one instance, the hopper was wired to a clock which made the hopper available to the pigeon for a five second period every 15 seconds. The appearance of the hopper was in no way contingent upon what the pigeon did. Yet when pigeons were placed in this circumstance for a few minutes each day, some of them developed complex and often bizarre patterns of behavior. For example, one bird was reported to thrust its head repeatedly toward one upper corner of the cage between reinforcements. Another made counterclockwise turns around the cage, making two or three turns between reinforcements. To an observer, the correlation between the particular pattern of behavior and the reinforcement was not obvious. The bird appeared to be performing complex patterns of behavior to achieve food, even though neither the physical environment nor a trainer had established a causal link between the two.

Anyone with a pet animal is likely to become aware of similar accidental correlations. For example, most dogs prefer table scraps to regular dog food. One dog that is permitted fairly free opportunities to leave and reenter the house once found table scraps in her dish when she reentered the house. Now, during dish-washing time, if table scraps are not forthcoming, she asks to be let out, immediately asks to be readmitted, and promptly looks in her food dish for scraps.

These illustrations make clear that an accidental contingency of reinforcement coupled with the capacity of organisms to learn and to continue to perform behavior under intermittent reinforcement can combine to produce "superstitious" behavior. It is not difficult to find such patterns in our pets, our friends, and ourselves.

IMITATION AND MODELING

6

Many patterns of social behavior may be learned through two closely related processes called *imitation* and *modeling*.[1]

IMITATION

Imitation is not necessarily involved when the behavior of two organisms happens to be the same—the two may have learned the same behavior independently in the presence of the same cues. For this reason, one must know the conditions in which behavior was learned in order to know that it is truly imitative.

In order to study imitation, experimenters often construct a situation in which an organism is rewarded only when it imitates the behavior of another organism. Once the tendency to imitate is clearly established the subject can be tested to see if it will continue to imitate other organisms in situations far different from the one in which the original training was carried out. Those who study imitative behavior affirm that it is often a *generalized response* and that, once it is acquired, it will occur in a variety of situations.

The generality of imitation sets it apart from forms of learning that have been discussed previously. Even the most general of these, the acquisition of a learning "set," is conceived to be relevant only to a particular type of problem.

Miller and Dollard (1941), in their classic analysis of imitation, identify two ways in which behavior is learned through imitation: *copying* and *matched-dependent behavior*. In copying, the learner gradually brings his own performance into close approximation to that of a model. An example is instruction in handwriting as it was once given in the lower grades of school. The teacher provided the pupil with model handwriting, either in a book or on the blackboard, and the student copied the script over and over in an effort to reproduce it. In copying, it is possible for the subject to tell when he has produced an acceptable copy of a performance. By contrast, the subject is completely dependent

[1] Social learning is treated extensively in Zajonc, *Social Psychology: An Experimental Approach*, 1966, in this series.

upon the acts of the leader for cues as to what is appropriate in matched-dependent behavior. Miller and Dollard undertook to demonstrate this kind of learning in experiments with both rats and children.

The experimenters specified four necessary conditions for learning. According to them, there must be a *drive* which impels the organism to action. (According to Miller and Dollard, a drive is a strong stimulus, and any stimulus may become a drive, if it is strong enough.) There must be *cues* which determine when the organism will respond, where it will respond, and which response it will make. They also believed that the organism brings to the situation a hierarchy of *responses,* at least one of which must lead to reward, if the organism is to learn; *reward,* which Miller and Dollard equate with reinforcement, is defined as that stimulus or condition which reduces the intensity of the drive stimulus. Previously neutral stimuli may become acquired or secondary rewards through association, but a stimulus cannot be reinforcing except in the presence of the appropriate drive.

According to Miller and Dollard, the essential difference between matched-dependent learning and ordinary learning lies in the nature of the cue. This difference can be made clear in a simple experiment. Suppose a hungry rat, which we shall designate as the *leader,* is trained to choose one of two alternative paths to food on the basis of the location of a black, as opposed to a white, card. The drive is hunger; the cue is the black card; the appropriate response is turning in the direction indicated by the placement of the card; and the reward is food. Suppose we then train a *follower* to make either the same choice as the leader or the opposite choice. The drive, the response, and the reward will be the same, but the cue will be different. To attain the food reward, the follower animal must utilize the behavior of the leader rat as the *cue* for either imitation or "nonimitation." (Both imitation and nonimitation are forms of matched-dependent behavior.) This design was followed in the Miller and Dollard experiments, where the apparatus was an elevated maze. The maze had a short starting stem, and a gap separated the stem from two short runways, one leading right, the other left. At the ends of the two arms there were clips to hold the black and white cue cards and a sunken cup for the food reward for the leader animals. To reward imitative behavior, the experimenter could open small lids in the runway and expose food for the follower animals.

To establish that imitation was a generalized habit, it was necessary to train three different groups of leader rats. One group of eight albino rats were trained to discriminate between black and white cards. For four of the animals, the black card was positive and the white card was negative, and for the other four, the cues were reversed. The albinos were trained to discriminate between the black and white cards while the cards were shifted back and forth unpredictably so that the only cue available to the animal was the presence of the positive card on one of the arms. The rats usually required a large number of trials before they learned to discriminate essentially without error. Once these leader rats had learned to perform the task successfully alone, they were given some additional training with a following rat placed behind them on the starting stem at the beginning of each trial. This additional training was necessary to prevent the introduction of follower rats from disrupting the learned discrimination of the leaders.

For testing purposes, two more groups of leader rats were also trained. One was a group of eight albino rats and the second was a group of eight black rats. Both groups were trained to make a simple position response. Half of each group was trained to go to the left for food; half to go to the right.

Sixteen follower animals were then trained and tested in matched-dependent behavior. Half were trained to be imitators and the other half to be "nonimitators." A leader rat was placed on the starting stem and a follower was placed immediately behind him. If the follower rat was being trained to imitate, whenever he chose the side chosen by the leader rat, the experimenter raised the lid on the runway which exposed a food reward for the follower. If the follower was being trained to deviate from the leader's behavior, the reward was exposed only when he chose the side opposite to that of the leader. A trial was complete only when the follower made a correct choice. If the follower made a wrong turn, both the follower and the leader were restored to the starting stem and the process repeated until a correct choice occurred. The training consisted of seven such trials a day for each animal for 12 days, or a total of 84 training trials. Only the first run in each trial was scored as being either correct or incorrect. Thus each animal could achieve a score for the day ranging from 0 to 7. Since there were eight imitators and eight non-imitators, and each had seven trials per day, there were 56 trials a day for each group. The results of this training are shown in Figure 6.1. It is obvious that in the 12 days of training, the imitators had learned to do whatever the leader did, and the "nonimitators" had learned to do the opposite.

However, one could question whether the follower rats had learned to imitate or counterimitate or had simply learned to make the same discrimination between the cards that served the leader rats as cues. Even though 84 trials are usually insufficient for an animal to make the black/white discrimination, the follower rats may have been aided in making this discrimination by the presence of the leader rat. Indeed they may have, but the question is really whether they can respond appropriately to a leader rat, when such a leader is the only available cue.

Three tests of the follower rats' acquired tendency to imitate or not imitate were then arranged. In the first test, the black cards and white

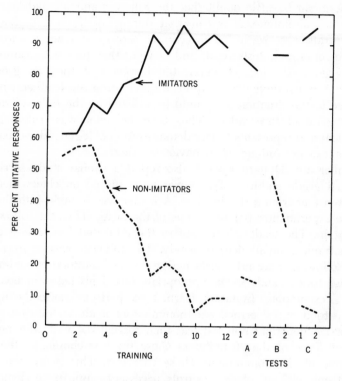

PER CENT IMITATIVE RESPONSES

← IMITATORS

← NON-IMITATORS

TRAINING

TESTS

A   B   C

Figure 6.1

*Curves showing the learning and testing of imitation
and "nonimitation" in rats. See text for description of
the three test procedures. (Drawn from Miller and
Dollard, 1941. Copyright 1941 by The Yale University Press. Drawn by permission of the authors and
publisher.)*

cards were removed, and new leader rats were substituted from the group
of albino rats that had been trained in position habits. The follower rats
were given seven test trials a day for two days, being first placed behind
left-turning and then right-turning leaders in an unpredictable fashion.
The only cue available for a correct response in this situation was the
behavior of the leader rat. This test is designated test *A* in Figure 6.1.
In test *B*, also consisting of seven trials a day for two days, left-turning
and right-turning *black* rats were substituted for the albinos so that the
experimenters could be sure that imitation and nonimitation were not specific to white leaders. Test *C* was carried out for two days with the same
white rats used in test *A*, but with thirst motivation rather than hunger.
The results of the three tests are shown in the right half of Figure 6.1.

There can be little doubt that the follower animals had learned to imitate or not imitate. It is true that during all three test phases the follower rats were rewarded for correct choices and not rewarded for incorrect ones, and tests A, B, and C were therefore not unambiguous tests of generalization. However, the behavior of the two groups of follower rats continued to be quite different from each other when the only cue in the situation that could be utilized by the follower rats was the behavior of the leaders. Thus their behavior was truly matched-dependent and represents a clear demonstration of a generalized tendency to imitate or not imitate the behavior of others.

Miller and Dollard (1941) also report a similar study carried out with first grade children. Two boxes were placed on chairs in a room about ten feet from a starting line. A leader was brought into the room and the experimenter pointed to one of the boxes. Then the follower was brought in. The leader then went to the indicated box, raised the lid, and took out a small piece of candy. The follower was then given his turn. Followers were arbitrarily designated as imitators or nonimitators, and each found candy in the appropriate box if his behavior conformed to his designation. Imitators learned to perform perfectly with an average total of 1.7 errors, and nonimitators made an average of only .4 errors. A generalization test was then carried out with four boxes. In this test, 75% of the 20 imitators chose the box chosen by the leader and none of the nonimitators chose that box. This study, which was carried out with all of the controls necessary, appears to demonstrate that the paradigm for matched-dependent behavior could also be used successfully with children.

What are the implications of such laboratory experiments for every-day human behavior? Imitation is a very general kind of response for which there are highly available cues. In imitation, we may find a paradigm for learning generalized ways of behaving in a wide variety of everyday situations. The reader who is interested in a fuller treatment of theories concerning the role of imitation in human behavior and other experiments with both human and animal subjects should see the extensive appendix of Miller and Dollard (1941). Some aspects of this experiment with first grade children are also discussed in Zajonc (1966).

MODELING

Modeling is similar to imitation in terms of the experimental arrangements, except that the emphasis of modeling is on the production of a novel response by the organism. Thus, in modeling, considerable information is given the organism to make the desired response likely. If one is dealing with a verbal organism, it is often possible through verbal instruction to induce that organism to perform a response that would have a zero probability of occurrence without the instruction. However, when one is dealing with a nonverbal organism or when the circumstances are such that verbal information simply cannot be provided or is undesirable, modeling offers a means of providing a stimulus containing far more information than is provided in any other learning procedure discussed in this volume. In the paradigm of modeling, the model performs a complex response in the presence of the organism to be trained, and the modeled behavior is rewarded when the response occurs.

A number of demonstrations of modeling as a learning procedure have been developed by Bandura. He has made an effort to analyze the manner in which the modeled behavior comes to be copied by the observer, and he has found reason to suggest revisions in the nature and significance of some of the basic concepts of learning theory.

When an observer copies the behavior of a model, according to Bandura (Bandura and Walters, 1964; Bandura, 1965), three possible means of bringing about the novel response in the observer may be involved: (1) The response may be simply *elicited* in the observer. This occurs when the observer already has the complete response pattern immediately available. The effect of the model is only to facilitate the occurrence of the response. (2) A new response pattern may be induced by strengthening or weakening response elements that are already present, resulting in the emergence of a new pattern of behavior. (3) The observer may acquire a new response that did not exist in the response repertoire, although the new response is certainly composed of previously learned or available elements. Thus the novel character of the response stems from the particular combination of elements.

In one study, Bandura and McDonald (1963) undertook to demonstrate the superiority of modeling to the simple shaping procedures of operant conditioning. In this study, young children were given stories relating well-intentioned acts with drastic consequences and maliciously motivated acts with minor consequences. They were to judge which was the "naughtier thing." They were then induced to make moral evaluative statements counter to their own under three conditions. In one condition, they observed adult models who expressed moral judgments, and the children were reinforced for making similar judgments. In a second condition, they observed the adult models but the children were not reinforced. In the third condition, no models were provided, but the children were reinforced for making moral evaluative statements exactly as they were in the first condition. This study is discussed in some detail in Zajonc (1966), but for present purposes, it is sufficient to note that observation of the model, with or without reinforcement, produced far more change in the behavior of the children than did simple reinforcement alone. Bandura argues that the method of successive approximation, as a means of shaping behavior, is inefficient compared to modeling. In the method of successive approximation, the only source of useful information is the contingency of reinforcement. In modeling, the behavior of the model is a relatively rich source of information for the observer.

The use of modeling as a training procedure has suggested two revisions in the conceptualization of the learning process. These have been emphasized by Bandura (1965). Since there is both a model and an "observer" in the situation, one has the options of rewarding or punishing the model, the observer, or both. Rewarding or punishing the model, in contrast to the observer, is called *vicarious* reinforcement. One can well ask what effect vicarious reinforcement of the model has on the behavior of the observer, even when no reinforcement is applied to the behavior of the observer.

A second theoretical issue stressed by Bandura (1965) is the role of reinforcement in producing learning, as distinguished from its role in producing performance. Miller and Dollard (1941) are representative of a large group of learning theorists who make the assumption that learning does not occur without the application of reinforcement. Indeed, in operant conditioning, as promulgated by Skinner (1938, 1953), reinforcement is the only significant variable that modifies behavior. Bandura disagrees with this position. In contemplating a situation in which a human subject is the passive recipient of verbal instruction or a situation in which the behavior of a model is provided as a source of complex information for the observer, Bandura concludes that reinforcement is not necessary for *learning*. The observer *learns* the response without either performing it or being reinforced for that performance. Bandura characterizes traditional reinforcement theory as assuming that the observer suspends learning until the reinforcement arrives, however long that delay is. Bandura conceives of reinforcement as having an influence only on the *performance* or *nonperformance* of the response *after* it is learned.

Bandura (1965) has attempted to demonstrate both the efficacy of vicarious reinforcement and the distinction between the role of reinforcement in modifying performance and the role of reinforcement in modifying learning. In this experimental demonstration, three groups of children each observed film in which a model exhibited novel physical and verbal aggressive responses. Vicarious reinforcement was manipulated by establishing three different conditions with three different films. In one condition, the model was generously rewarded for its aggressive behavior. In a second condition, the model was severely punished. In the third condition, no consequences were shown for the model's behavior. After the children had observed the behavior of the model and the consequences, they were given performance tests for aggressive behavior. In these tests, the instances in which they performed imitative behavior were recorded. No reinforcement was applied to the behavior of the children in this phase. The effects of vicarious reinforcement may be seen in Figure 6.2 in the "no incentive" condition. There was little difference between the condition in which the model was rewarded and the condition in which no

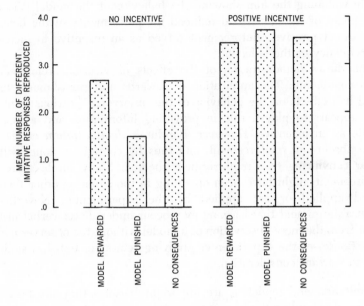

Figure 6.2

*Mean number of different imitative responses repro-
duced by children on the basis of modeling experience in which model was rewarded, punished, or
suffered no consequences for its behavior. In the
"no incentive" condition, the children received no
reinforcement for imitation behavior. In the "positive
incentive" condition, the children had been offered
highly attractive incentives for reproducing the model's responses. (Redrawn and simplified from Bandura,
1965. Copyright 1965 by Holt, Rinehart and Win-
ston, Inc. Reproduced by permission of the authors
and publisher.)*

consequences for the behavior were shown, but the effects of punishment of the model were apparent. Vicarious punishment reduced the frequency of imitative behavior.

Bandura contends that the children had *learned* the aggressive behavior by observing the model and that the vicarious reinforcement had influenced their performance in the later tests. A further demonstration was provided in a third session in which highly attractive incentives (reinforcement) were offered the children for the performance of imitative behavior. The frequency of imitative responses increased in all three groups of children, with the largest increase occurring in that group of children who observed the model receiving punishment for the aggressive behavior. Bandura argues that these children had learned by merely watching the film showing the behavior of the model. Vicarious punishment of the model had reduced the performance of the behavior, while direct positive reinforcement served as an incentive in increasing the frequency of the behavior.

Bandura's demonstration of the effects of vicarious reinforcement seems convincing. The application of rewards and punishments to the model had effects on the behavior of the observers. Vicarious reinforcement appears to play a role in providing information and appears to operate as an incentive. However, Bandura's *demonstration* of learning in the absence of reinforcement, and thus by contiguity alone, will not appear convincing to a reinforcement theorist. Many subtle sources of reinforcement might have been operating in the situation other than the reward applied or not applied by the experimenter. Nevertheless, Bandura's argument that learning may occur under direct verbal instruction or from the mere observation of a model without the observer making the response—or the experimenter applying reinforcement—has sufficient merit to warrant consideration.

Imitation and modeling are important because they illustrate possibilities of extending the learning principles described in earlier chapters to very generalized kinds of responses that are applicable in many situations and to situations in which a complex stimulus is needed in order to induce a correct response. Thus, these principles of learning can be extended to account for everyday learning. To some degree, we have all learned to imitate and also to model our behavior after those who perform successfully.

There is a growing tendency among psychologists who work in the field of learning to employ mathematical models to summarize findings and to substitute for theories couched in nonmathematical language. This development is sufficiently extensive and important that the most elementary treatment of experimental and theoretical developments in learning should include an introduction to at least two or three types of mathematical models of learning and to some of the language used in this context.

A MATHEMATICAL MODEL AS A SUMMARY OF EMPIRICAL DATA

Let us explore a simple illustration of the use of a mathematical model as a summary of findings. Suppose that we carry out a study in which a group of animals is induced to learn a complex maze problem to obtain pellets of food. We arrange to have the animals go without food for 22 hours before each daily training session, and we use four small pellets as a reward on each trial. Let us choose to take running speed as the measure. We might have chosen to use the number of errors, but our maze is a long and complex one. If an animal makes an error, it will increase the amount of time he takes to run the maze and thus reduce his speed. Furthermore, even after he learns to run without error, additional progress can be shown through further increases in speed. We might choose to measure speed by taking the reciprocal of the running time (1/time in seconds) so that the speed score will increase as running time decreases.

The data collected in this manner will then consist of a number of scores. If we train 50 animals and run each animal on 10 trials on each of 10 days, we shall accumulate 5,000 scores. One way to begin to summarize the data is to take the average score for each of the hundred trials by adding the individual scores of each of the 50 animals and dividing by 50. We have now reduced the 5,000 individual scores to 100 mean scores. We have a record of the progress of the *group* in learning the problem. In the process we have lost the record of individual animals. It is also frequently true that in averaging the scores, an additional assumption is made: that the learning process in each individual animal is essentially the same as that in any other animal. Thus if we plot a graph of mean scores by trials, the curve will be assumed to reflect the character of the learning process in each and every animal.

Suppose that the curve we have obtained is somewhat irregular, rising in general, but showing some reversal in its progress. In order to achieve a smoother curve, we might choose to take a mean of successive blocks of 10 trials, and thus a mean of all of the trials run on each day of the experiment. We shall now have reduced our 5,000 scores to 10 values—a very condensed summary. It is frequently true that in order to justify this last step, it is assumed that the irregularities in the previously plotted curve were due to the operation of chance factors.

We now plot a curve such as that in Figure 7.1. It has only 10 points, and when they are connected, we observe that it is a fairly smooth curve that rises rapidly at first and then levels off. It is easy to conclude from

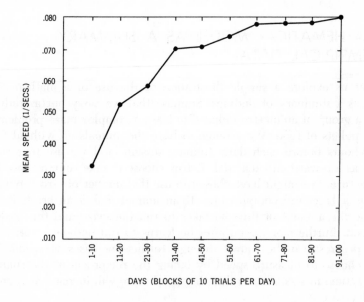

Figure 7.1

Plot of mean speed scores from hypothetical experiment (see text for explanation).

the shape of the curve that the learning process grows rapidly at first and shows progressively less improvement as practice continues. Notice, however, that we have reached this conclusion on the basis of an abstract of the original data. To attain the level of abstraction represented by the plot of the ten points in Figure 7.1, theorists often make two strong assumptions: (1) the learning process is the same in all animals, and, (2) variation in scores can be attributed to chance factors. It is quite possible that neither assumption is wholly justified. Furthermore, in the process of abstraction, we threw away a large amount of information. From the 10 means alone we could not recover the original data.

After examining the curve (Figure 7.1), we might want to try another method of reducing the mass of 5,000 scores to a simple abstraction. We might decide to fit a curve to the 10 means by one of several curve-fitting procedures that are only slightly more complex than the process of obtaining means across animals and then means across blocks of 10 trials.

The first step is to find a type of equation that fits the general pattern exhibited by curves we obtained by the first process. A number of equations might be used in fitting the data. One of these is a simple exponential equation. We might select this particular equation partly because it happens to fit many sets of data obtained by measuring the process of physical growth. In fact, it is sometimes referred to as the "growth equation." One form of exponential equation that proves to fit the data fairly well is the following:

$$Z = x\,(1 - 10^{-uT}). \tag{1}$$

The relation of the various values in the equation to the learning process—as shown in the curve we obtained before—may also be seen in Figure 7.2. Z is the measure of performance, in this case, speed. T is the ordinal number of the trial. Both Z and T are empirical variables for which we obtained values in the original experiment. The x in the equation is a value obtained in the curve-fitting process, and it expresses the maximum performance we might expect to obtain if training was to be carried on indefinitely. Thus x is the asymptote, the maximum value of the curve at infinity—a theoretical limit the curve constantly approaches. The u in the equation is also a value obtained in the process of curve-fitting. It expresses the rate of learning or, in other words, the rapidity with which the curve approaches the asymptote. It is the fraction remaining of the distance to x that will be gained in a trial. If u is constant, the gain will be smaller on each successive trial because the remaining distance to the asymptote, x, is smaller. The operation of u is indicated in the figure only indirectly by the constant proportional but different absolute amounts of gain between the first two data points as contrasted with the gain between the second and third points. If u is large, the curve will rise sharply at the beginning. If u is small, the curve will appear flatter and will approach the asymptote more slowly. The 10 in the equation reflects the fact that logarithms to the base 10 are to be employed in the curve-fitting process.[1]

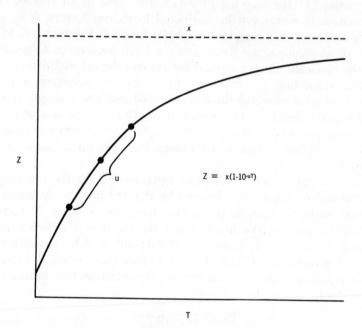

Figure 7.2

Graphic form of Equation 1 (see text for explanation).

It should be noted that u is firmly identified with *learning* and x is firmly identified with *performance*. Learning is defined as the change in performance that occurs with experience. In expressing ultimate performance, x should be identified with those variables in a learning problem that remain constant. Whether some experimental manipulations change u, x, or both, remains an empirical question.

If we fit the data of Figure 7.1 to Equation 1 to obtain appropriate numbers to represent x and u, the result might be the equation in Figure 7.3. Since we have obtained values for x and u, it is now possible to choose any value we wish for T, then solve for Z. We can calculate a number of Z values and plot a smooth curve to represent the learning process. The result will appear as the curve in Figure 7.3. The curve and the equation are both simple abstractions from the data, and as such are simple summaries of the data, very much as the plot of mean values in Figure 7.1 is an abstraction and summary.

[1] For a programmed introduction to common logarithms, see Lane and Bem, *A Laboratory Manual for the Control and Analysis of Behavior*, 1965, in this series.

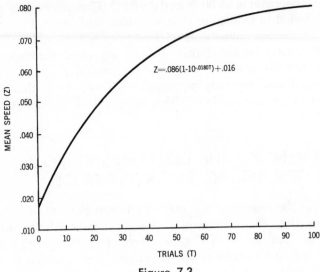

Figure 7.3

Exponential equation resulting from fitting a curve to the data plotted in Figure 7.1 (see text for explanation).

It should be noted, however, that in choosing the exponential or growth equation, we have made at least one further assumption about the learning process. While it may not be obvious, we have made the assumption that learning is a continuous process rather than a discrete one. We have borrowed from the calculus the underlying assumption of continuity. From the equation, it is possible to calculate the performance on trial 17.6 even though .6 of a trial makes no sense. The equation permits us to extrapolate the curve back to zero training or even beyond to negative values of training. In essence, in choosing this equation form and in making the relevant assumptions, we have denied the possibility that learning proceeds in an all-or-nothing fashion or that it proceeds in finite and discrete steps. Alternative equation forms might have been chosen that involve quite different assumptions; one of these alternatives will be discussed later.

One may regard either the formal verbal statements that result in the formulation of Equation 1 or the equation itself as a mathematical model of the learning process—it is a summarizing model to the extent that we use it only to summarize a set of data. But it is rarely used as a simple summary. More commonly the mathematical assumptions involved in summarizing are transferred to the learning process itself. We have made at least three very strong assumptions: (1) that the learning process is essentially the same in all 50 animals,[1] (2) that irregularities in progress can be attributed to random or chance factors, and (3) that the learning process is continuous (sometimes referred to as incremental) rather than discrete. It should be noted that verbally expressed learning theories frequently involve similar strong assumptions that are not clearly expressed—and are frequently unrecognized. Thus, one of the virtues of building mathematical models is that assumptions frequently become more explicit.

DEVELOPMENT OF THE DETERMINISTIC MODEL INTO A GENERALIZED, PREDICTIVE MODEL

A part of the usefulness of a mathematical model will be determined by its generality. There are two ways we can proceed to explore the generality of Equation 1 as a general model of the learning process. Since it is only a summary of the data from one experiment, we may wish to prove that the values we obtained are reliable estimates. We can repeat the identical experiment a number of times, fitting curves to each new set of data until we become convinced that our values are reliable estimates of the rate of learning and the ultimate performance to be expected. This procedure is not trivial, but it is uninteresting.

A more interesting path to generality is to explore what happens to x and u when we deliberately change the nature of the experiment, or vary one of the conditions of learning. Suppose that we decide to run another group of 50 animals with the conditions exactly the same except that instead of being deprived of food for 22 hours during the training, they are deprived for only three hours and can therefore be assumed to be less hungry. If we then employ the new set of data, we might obtain the lower curve shown in Figure 7.4. The most obvious difference between the two curves is the big difference in running speed that the two groups seem to have adopted. This difference is reflected in the difference between .086 and .045 as estimates of x. It is obvious, therefore, that the difference in deprivation level between the two groups resulted in different levels of *performance*. On the other hand, the fact that the two estimates of u, reflecting the rate of *learning*, are essentially identical seems to establish that the difference in deprivation level did *not* affect the *rate of learning*. Furthermore, the estimate of the constant at the end of each equation is the same, and this has another interesting implication. Since the constant, in this case .016, indicates the point at

---

[1]An assumption even more firmly grounded by the fact that if the animals learned at different rates, curves of individual performance could be fit by exponential equations, but a curve that is an average of exponential curves with different exponents is not an exponential curve.

which the curve reaches zero on the abscissa—a point which reflects running speed before there is any training—the identity of this value in the two equations implies that initial running speed did not differ

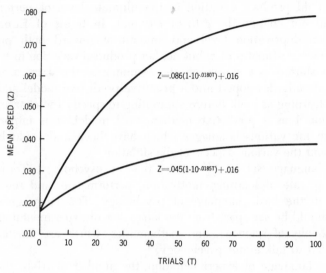

$$Z = .086(1 - 10^{-.0180T}) + .016$$

$$Z = .045(1 - 10^{-.0185T}) + .016$$

MEAN SPEED (Z)

TRIALS (T)

Figure 7.4

Exponential equations resulting from fitting curves to two sets of hypothetical data acquired under two different times of food deprivation (see text for explanation).

between the two. It is thus implied that the difference in deprivation level did not produce a difference in "general activity" or, more strictly, the time taken to get from the start to the goal box before the animals had experienced the food incentive.

While data on which Figure 7.4 is based are purely hypothetical and the equations in the figure are fabrications, the results are not at all unlikely. Furthermore, rather than vary the time of deprivation, we might have chosen to vary the amount of reward. In the original experiment we described conditions of training as involving 22 hours of deprivation of food, and four small pellets reward on each trial. We might have run still a third group with the same time of deprivation, 22 hours, but with only one small pellet as a reward on each trial. It is quite possible that the data would be fit by the following values in the equation:

$$Z = .058 \ (1 - 10^{-.0183T}) + .016).$$

If we had actually obtained such values, and again the result is a quite possible one, we would have noted that both the origin of the curve and the rate of approach to the asymptote did not differ materially from similar values in Figure 7.4, but that the estimate of the asymptote, .058, was different. We should then conclude that variation in the amount of reward would produce variation in the ultimate level of *performance*, but would not change the rate of *learning*. In terms of Equation 1, variation in deprivation level and amount of reward both produced variation in the estimates of x, but neither produced variation in u.

What started as a simple effort to summarize the data in equation form has already developed into a primitive predictive model and into a theory of learning as well. Before attempting to specify the characteristics of Equation 1 as a predictive mathematical model, it is important to distinguish the various languages which have been and could be used to talk about the various aspects of the situation.

One language set is, of course, that of psychology. Terms such as learning, rate of learning, motivation, performance, and reward are included in the basic language of psychology. The language of psychology should be set apart from the languages of experimentation, logic (or philosophy of science), and mathematics, which are ancillary languages used to talk *about* psychology.

In the language of experimentation, the number of trials, the hours of deprivation, and the amount of the incentive are all *independent* variables, while the running speed is a *dependent* variable. The first three terms specify the arrangements of conditions we made to put the question to nature. The dependent variable, running speed, is nature's answer.

In the language of logic (or philosophy of science), the Z and T of Equation 1 are empirical or observable constructs; capital letters are used to indicate this status. The T is a manipulated variable, because it is under the direct control of the experimenter. Z, on the other hand, is a *performance* variable because it is the empirically measured performance. The u and x of Equation 1 are essentially *theoretical* constructs, and most often are *intervening* variables. They are printed in lower case to distinguish them from more directly measured empirical constructs. Figure 7.5 shows these relationships. Solid lines in the diagram indicate that the necessary connections between empirical and theoretical constructs, namely, appropriate *coordinating definitions*, are implicit in the equation. It is also true that the equation form establishes the necessary *implicit definition* which relates x and u. Further discussion of the language of the philosophy of science can be found in another volume in this series (Walker, *Psychology as a Natural and Social Science*, pending).

In our discussion of the hypothetical experiment, two values of x were established on the basis of two values of time of deprivation of food, three and 22 hours. Furthermore, it was assumed that we might expect to obtain two values of x with two different amounts of food reward. If we designate H to stand for hours of deprivation, and R to stand for the amount of reward, it would be possible to write quotations which related H and R to x and Z in which u was found to be unaffected and thus a constant. Only a linear equation could be fit to either, since we

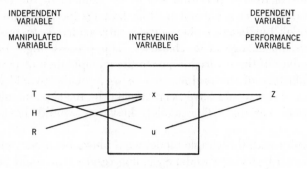

Figure 7.5

Diagram showing the correspondence between the language of experimentation, the language of logic or philosophy of science, and the variables of Equation 1 (see text for explanation).

had obtained only two values for each variable. Obtaining data for other values of H and R would improve our knowledge of the shape of the relationship and our confidence in statements concerning the shape, but would not change the character of the logical relationships between empirical constructs and their associated theoretical counterparts.

If Equation 1 is to be used as a predictive mathematical model, then the discussion is to be carried on in the fourth language, that of mathematics. In that language, T, Z, x, and u are all *variables* because they can assume a variety of values. In addition, x and u are called *parameters*. Equation 1 might have been written with the value $+c$ as a terminal member. It is a *constant* in the curve-fitting process as the value of the point at which the curve crosses the ordinate.

While Equation 1 as a summarizing model started with a set of data and continued an abstraction from it, the same equation as a predictive mathematical model is an abstraction from which one predicts data. The interest in mathematical models of learning arises from a consideration of the mathematical properties of the model itself. The model is taken as fixed, and the effort is to generalize it as far as possible without giving up its essential character. As indicated previously, Equation 1 can be generalized in two or more ways. The experiment can be repeated and the curve-fitting process carried out repeatedly until one is confident that the obtained values for x, u, and c are stable values. The curve may be extrapolated to values of T that were not tried, such as 200 or 1,000 trials. Then predictions may be made from the model concerning the values of Z, the performance, for these values of T. Finally, empirical tests of the prediction may be made. A third procedure would involve the manipulation of other empirical constructs. We discussed the manipulation of time of food deprivation and of the amount of the reward. Both were found to affect x but not u. Both findings increased the generality of the model, but because they gave a satisfactory fit to the data, they did not force a change in its character. This process might be extended to other values of these variables, or to the manipulation of new variables, such as difficulty of the problem where we probably would have found that both x and u would have been affected by the same manipulation of an empirical variable. The model, however, would have remained inviolate.

Difficulty with this simple model would have been encountered if we had happened to try a procedure yielding results that could not be fit by a simple exponential equation. For example, suppose that we had actually tested the model at 1,000 trials and found that, instead of approaching more and more closely to the asymptote, the curve began to fall. Or suppose we constructed a difficult problem and found a curve that rose to an apparent maximum value and then, after an extended period of no apparent change, began to rise once again. Only then would it have been necessary to reconsider the nature of the model itself, since such results could not be fit by an exponential equation.

THE STIMULUS SAMPLING MODEL

The irregularities in the behavior of individual animals and their unsteady progress toward their ultimate performance levels were assumed to be attributable to uncontrolled, random, or chance factors and were not taken explicitly into account in the *deterministic* model. To mathematically oriented people, the irregularities suggest the operation of *probabilistic* as opposed to deterministic processes. If one views the irregularity in performance as the basic characteristic of the behavior, then one might prefer to choose a *stochastic* or probabilistic model. Stochastic models are statistical in character and involve uncertainty in outcome as opposed to the certainty involved in deterministic models.

A prominent example of a stochastic learning theory is the *stimulus sampling* theory of Estes (1959). This theory makes use of the mathematics of set theory and probability theory in combination. While Estes' theory, in its mathematical form, is complex and highly developed, a few simple elements of it can be extracted to demonstrate some of the characteristics and properties of stochastic models.

The verbal statement of the essence of Estes' learning theory is simple. It is the elaboration of the stochastic model that becomes complex. From the standpoint of the model, the stimulus universe can be conceived of as composed of elemental stimuli. The response universe may likewise be conceived of as a large population of elements. Both stimuli and responses are thought of in terms of sets and subsets of elements with the connections between them described in probabilistic terms. Both learning (the change in connections between stimulus elements and a response) and performance (the production of a response on any given trial) are described in terms of probabilities. Estes' theory is built on five simple postulates or propositions, which are obviously chosen because of their mathematical properties. Rephrased from Estes (1959) they are:

Response. The entire universe of responses is divided into mutually exclusive and exhaustive categories. Each category is described as a subset and is characterized as having a probability of occurrence. The probabilities of the subsets sum to 1.00.

Stimulus-Response Relations. The stimulus set is partitioned by the responses to which the elements are attached. Every element of the stimulus set is attached to one and only one response. Probability of response is equal to the proportion of the elements attached to the response in question.

Learning. All elements present on a trial on which the response occurs and is reinforced are thereby connected to the response. If the element is not present, or if no reinforcement occurs, there is no learning, no change in connection.

Stimulus Fluctuation. Gradual learning and response variability are both accounted for in terms of the statement that only a portion of the stimuli which might be sampled is actually sampled on a given trial. Furthermore, the exchange between the set sampled and the set momentarily unavailable for sampling requires time.

Stimulus Sampling. To every element of s is associated a probability of being sampled, θ.

In Estes' model, the definition of reinforcement is implicit in the postulates. For each response class there exists a class of events which are reinforcing. There is no independent definition of reinforcement. Whichever event is found to increase the probability of the evocation of a response in the presence of a given stimulus set is, by this definition, a reinforcing event.

The full stimulus sampling model as described in Estes (1959) has at least 19 variables or theoretical terms. A minimum of eight is necessary to develop a simple formula for a learning curve similar to Equation 1. Here are the eight terms:

S = the total set of stimulus elements.

s = the mean stimulus sample size. Thus s is a subset of S and a recognition of the condition that only a subset of the total stimulus set will be present on any given trial.

N = the number of elements in S.

θ_i = the probability that the ith element (any given element) will be sampled on any given trial.

A_j = a set of r mutually exclusive and exhaustive response classes.

E_k = a set of reinforcing events, one [event] corresponding to each response class.

n = the ordinal number of the trial.

p_n = the probability of A_j on trial n in the presence of the stimulus situation, S.

In order to generate a smooth curve of the kind which is characteristic of Equation 1, it is necessary to make several strong, limiting assumptions. Some of the differences between the deterministic and the stochastic models may become clear from this process. One assumption might be that all θ values are the same. θ_i is the probability that a given stimulus element will be sampled, and the probability of sampling can differ between elements. However, if we make the assumption that all elements of S are equally likely to be sampled, the θ will be equal for all elements. If, in addition, we deal with mean values of θ, then the size of s will be precisely determined by θ. Since N is the number of elements in S, then

$$s = N\theta.$$

An even stronger assumption may be made concerning p. While θ concerns the size of the sample of S drawn on each trial, p represents the proportion of that sample which is associated with A_j through previous reinforcements. To generate a smooth curve, it is necessary to assume that the proportion of the sample drawn on each trial that is connected to A_j is identical to the proportion of the total population, S, that is associated with A_j. Given these assumptions, Equation 2,

$$p_n = 1 - (1 - \theta_i)^n, \tag{2}$$

can be used to generate a smooth curve. It should be noted that because of these restrictive assumptions, the lefthand term of the equation could have been either $N\theta$ or s, since both have been made equal to p by our assumptions. If we choose .5 as a value for θ, for the sake of simplicity, then a series of values can be calculated for p by solving Equation 2 for a series of values of n. Figure 7.6 is a plot of values for p through five trials. It can be seen that in this instance the curve that is generated has properties that are identical to the curve generated by Equation 1. Because the curve rises to an absolute limit of a probability of 1.0, the

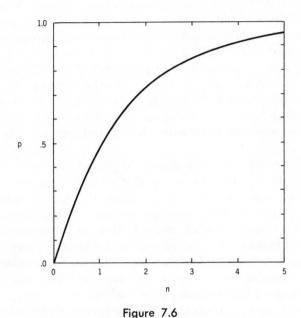

Figure 7.6

Graphic plot of solutions for Equation 2 for six values of n (see text for explanataion).

value 1 in Equation 2 is an asymptote just as x described the asymptote in Equation 1. The rate of rise to the asymptote is determined in Equation 2 by the quantity $(1 - \theta_i)^n$, which decreases as n increases, changing the value of p_n by a fixed fraction of the remaining distance to the asymptote just as the curve generated in the case of Equation 1 proceeded with successive units of training by a fixed fraction of the remaining distince to x as defined by the exponent, uT. It should be noted that Estes' model can be developed to deal with other dependent variables, such as latency of response, in which the asymptote is free to vary with the conditions of the experiment and is not arbitrarily limited, as is true when probability of response is the performance term.

The fact that the two equations are mathematically identical arises from the restrictive assumptions that were made. Without them, Equation 2 describes not only the mean values of the learning curve, but the distribution of values to be expected. The increase in the proportion of the S population associated with the response would depend on the number of unassociated elements that happen to be in the particular sample of elements, s. Furthermore, the performance would not necessarily be an exact reflection of the amount of learning. If a particular sample set was unrepresentative of the proportion of learned connections, the performance might reflect a proportion that is greater or lesser than the actual proportion of connected elements. Thus, without the restrictive assumptions, a curve plotted from Equation 2 would rise irregularly unless a sufficient number of calculations were made from the equation, in a manner equivalent to running a large number of animals, so that neither the rate of learning nor the degree of representation of learning in performance departed from a mean value. It should be clear from this discussion that Estes' stimulus sampling model makes a clear distinction between learning, as represented by θ, and performance, as represented by p.

The difference between learning and performance in the Estes' model can be further expanded by noting that while learning may proceed in one direction only, performance can show reversals of direction. This condition follows, in part, from the postulate that connections remain unchanged if there is no reinforcement. Thus, in a learning situation, the number of elements of S connected to the response may increase in varying amounts from trial to trial depending on the number of unconnected elements in the sample, s. But they may not decrease. To the extent that the particular sample, s, underestimates the proportion of elements in S that are connected to the response, there exists the possibility of a drop in the performance curve.

It should also be noted that a curve generated from Equation 2 can depart from the simple exponential form in a number of ways. One example might involve the assumption that some elements of S are readily available for sampling, while others are markedly less available. The result would be a performance curve that rises sharply and then proceeds over the remaining distance at a leisurely pace. The same curve could be fit with an exponential equation only by developing a more complex expression for the exponent.

As stated earlier, a basic and fundamental difference between the two models that have been discussed is the fact that the deterministic model assumes that the learning process is continuous, while the stochastic model, of which Estes' stimulus sampling model is an example, permits learning to proceed in discrete steps. A deterministic model predicts mean values, while the stochastic model describes the distribution of performance scores to be expected as well.

Thus, under certain restrictive assumptions and with a large number of elements, Estes' model can appear to behave as does a deterministic model. However, Estes' model can be made to deal with many kinds of data that would be difficult for a deterministic model. Furthermore, the development and application of such stochastic models have led to ingenious experimentation.

It is not a characteristic of mathematical models of learning, as such, but it is a characteristic of psychologists who build mathematical models of learning, that the model tends to become more important than the data. One can become quite interested in mathematical models of learning in a general sense and expend great effort in developing their properties. This interest can be accompanied by varying amounts of interest in data ranging from none at all to sufficient interest to produce strong programs of research, such as is the case with Estes and his students. However, when theories are cast in mathematical terms, there is a general tendency for the relationships between theoretical and empirical variables to be somewhat less formal than is likely to be the case with nonmathematical learning theories.

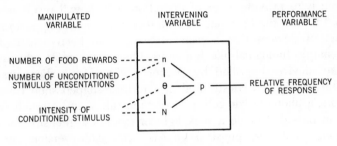

MANIPULATED VARIABLE

INTERVENING VARIABLE

PERFORMANCE VARIABLE

NUMBER OF FOOD REWARDS

NUMBER OF UNCONDITIONED STIMULUS PRESENTATIONS

INTENSITY OF CONDITIONED STIMULUS

RELATIVE FREQUENCY OF RESPONSE

Figure 7.7

Diagram of some of the interrelationships between theoretical constructs and the data level in Estes' stimulus sampling theory (see text for explanation).

Figure 7.7 is a diagram of a few of the concepts we have just discussed. Estes' theory has no empirical constructs as such. The four symbols in the box, as well as the remainder of the 19 symbols listed in Estes (1959), are all theoretical variables. The solid lines in the diagram represent the fact that the implicit definitions between theoretical terms are completely specified in the mathematical relationships indicated in the formula employed by Estes, of which Equation 2 is one example. As indicated in the diagram, n may at one time be interpreted as referring to the number of food rewards, and at another time as referring to the number of unconditioned-stimulus presentations. Manipulation of the intensity of the conditioned stimulus may simultaneously increase the number of elements in S, in N, and in the sampling probability, θ. Thus the tendency of many theorists is to interpret the model rather directly in terms of data rather than to indicate formal empirical constructs and coordinating definitions between the constructs and the theoretical terms.

As is always the case with probabilities, p is an unrealized potential, and thus a theoretical term in the language of theory. Probability of response is usually evidenced in terms of frequencies, and the relationship between p and frequency of response is also a matter of "interpretation" rather than formal statement—it appears generally true that the relationship between a mathematical model and the performance variables relevant to it are no more rigorously stated than the relationships between the theoretical terms and the manipulated variables. The general weakness of relationship between theoretical terms and empirical variables is represented in Figure 7.7 by the broken lines connecting the two classes of variables.

COMPUTER SIMULATION OF LEARNING

Machines can be induced to simulate the learning process. All that is required is to provide a set of operations which will result in a performance that has the essential characteristics of a learning performance. A number of devices that appear to learn have been constructed to perform simple biological-like functions. One of the most amusing is a "turtle-like" device described by Walter (1951). An earlier version of this machine had been constructed of a tortoise-shaped shell containing two motors, a photoelectric cell, two vacuum tubes, and a touch contact. The circuit provided made it seek light of moderate intensity and avoid both strong light and physical objects. The later version contained additional circuitry to provide for simple learning, and Walter refers to this model as *Machina docilis*. A learning machine may be regarded as a specialized computer. One possible benefit from the stuntlike effort to construct such a machine is detailed in Walter's report. He wished to build an analog of simple conditioning. Since the machine was attracted to moderately intense light, he wished to induce it to be attracted to a whistle by repeated presentation of the whistle just before moderately intense light was presented. In order to accomplish this simple effect, he found it necessary to provide seven distinct operations. (1) The beginning of a specific stimulus had to be sharply distinguished from the absence of the stimulus—it was the change in the stimulus that was important rather than its presence. (2) The effects of the neutral stimulus had to be extended in time—the machine had to remember it long enough to make an association. (3) The relevant stimuli had to be mixed in such a way that simultaneous presence of effects could be detected. (4) The effects of the two stimuli had to be summated or integrated to form a consolidated stimulus. (5) The circuit had to be designed to activate memory only when the frequency of paired occurrence of the stimuli exceeded some value of chance coincidence of the two. (6) Memory was programmed to decrease in strength with the passage of time. (7) Provision was then made for the necessity of testing the correlation between the two stimuli in comparison with other stimuli. Each of these seven requirements was met by the construction of a circuit element to carry out the function. The circuits Walter used are illustrated in the original article (1951). A major benefit of such an effort is apparent in the list of the seven necessary characteristics. It was necessary for Walter to be highly analytical in designing a machine to perform what had appeared to be a simple learning process. Some of the complexities of conditioning became evident only when he tried to simulate it mechanically.

However, it isn't necessary actually to build a machine to simulate a learning organism. A calculator or computer can be used to make the simple arithmetic calculations necessary to determine the values of an equation without the specialized machinery needed to construct a *Machina docilis*. The construction of a computer program can be expected to force the writer of a program to be as analytical and specific about the nature of the process to be simulated as the construction of a learning machine forced Walter to be.

Computer simulation of psychological processes, such as learning and performance, can generally proceed in either of two ways. One can construct a mathematical model, usually stochastic, and use the computer to make arithmetic calculations; or one can construct an information processing model based on more flexible utilization of the computer's capacity to handle logical operations. Gregg and Simon (1966) refer to the latter alternative as the construction of a "process model." An exploration of process models will not be undertaken here, although it is possible that they may come to be the most fruitful employment of the computer in simulation.

One essential value of the computer as an instrument of simulation arises from its enormous speed of operation. In a matter of seconds, it can perform calculations which might take days if done by hand. In fact, the speed of the computer makes tasks of computation practical which would not even be considered if they had to be done without the computer.

For the purposes of illustration, the very simple computer model of learning was programmed and run on a large digital computer by S. H. Robinovitz. The program was devised to simulate rats learning to go to one side of a simple T maze for food reward. The tendency to go to each side was assumed to be equal, and thus to have a value of .500 at the outset in terms of probabilities. Since the behavior of rats in a T maze is variable, it was necessary to build variability into the probabilities of going to either side. It was arbitrarily decided to subject the momentary value of turning to either side to variation with a standard deviation of .200. Standard deviations were used because of the availability on the computer of a subroutine for calculation of the standard deviation which could be used as a part of the input, and a value of .200 was chosen to permit occasional errors even after the tendency to go to the rewarded side was quite strong. In essence, the computer was asked to make a random selection of a value for each tendency on each trial from a distribution of values around the mean value of each tendency. Then the computer was asked to decide, on the basis of the higher value, which way the animal might be expected to turn. Using this procedure, the animal would have made equal choices to the two sides over a long run if nothing happened to change the value of either tendency.

Side 1 was chosen as the side for the computer to reward. For the sake of simplicity, it was decided that the computer should learn nothing from an incorrect choice. Therefore, it was instructed to make no change in the value of the tendency to turn to Side 2 when Side 2 was actually chosen. On the other hand, the computer was instructed to reward the rat whenever it chose Side 1. In order to represent the effects of reinforcement, the computer was instructed to add to the probability of choosing Side 1 an amount to be calculated. This value was found by taking the difference between the existing value of Side 1 tendency and 1.0 (the asymptote), multiplying it by .015, and adding the product to the Side 1 value. This operation is identical to the process of increasing the value of performance in Equation 1 (Figure 7.2) and Equation 2 (Figure 7.6). The value, .015, should produce learning at a rate somewhat slower than that pictured in Figure 7.4 in which the relevant values were .0180 and .0185. Thus, each time the computer actually chose Side 1, the value of the tendency to go to Side 1 was increased at the relative expense of the value of the tendency to go to Side 2.

COMPUTER LANGUAGES

Communication with a computer involves the use of mutual languages, languages that can be understood by both the operator and the computer. The "operational core" of the computer is able to deal with only two symbols, 0 and 1. In order to make calculations in terms of decimal numbers, it is necessary to translate one number system into the other. In order to make it easy for the ordinary user, translating programs have been written which perform this function routinely. Furthermore, many of the operations the computer is asked to perform are needed repeatedly. Therefore, a library of operational instructions has been developed which the computer can be asked to use on the basis of a simple request without going through the details of writing the instructions each time someone wants a given and common operation performed. The symbols that tell the computer what to do, including the symbols asking it to perform common operations, form a language that the computer understands perfectly and that human operators can learn to use.

The simple learning model detailed above was programmed in the MAD language. MAD stands for Michigan Algorithm Decoder. An algorithm is a set of rules for solving a problem. The MAD language is not too difficult to learn and is a general computer language rather widely available.

Table 7.1 is the program in MAD that describes the problem detailed above. Some of it may look strange because it comes so close to normal English. However, there are differences. Some of them are: there are no lower case letters in MAD, spellings that appear odd have a function, and nonalphabetic symbols tend to mean very different things to the computer than they ordinarily mean on a printed page. The program was included here only to illustrate what one looked like, and the reader is not expected to understand it unless he learns the MAD language or already knows it.

The program in Table 7.1 will calculate the performance of one rat under the rules laid down above. Table 7.2 contains a part of the product of the calculations made for one rat. A total of 200 trials were run, and Table 7.2 contains the results for 60 of those trials. This simulated rat happened to choose the correct side four times in the first 10 trials, seven times in the second 10, nine times in the block from 51–60, eight in the block 91–100, eight in the block 141–150, and 10 in the final block of the run. The performance would not be atypical of a real rat if his motivation was not high and the reward was small.

Four simulated rats were run on the computer, and the results were combined for the four in blocks of 20 successive trials. The learning curve that resulted is shown in Figure 7.8. It can be seen from the figure that the results of the simple computer simulation are essentially indistinguishable from results which might have been obtained in an experiment involving four real rats. The speed of the computer is such that a total of 15.8 seconds were required to run this simulation, of which only 2.4 seconds were required for the actual processing of the 800 simulated trials.

The problem that was used to write the program was kept simple in order to provide an illustration of the nature of computer simulation. With a simple program, two virtues can be demonstrated. The first is the increase in clarity and precision of statement of the principles required to write a program. Vague statements cannot be programmed. The second virtue is also clear. It is important to know whether a particular set of simple principles will in fact produce results that are similar to actual experimental results.

However, the very simplicity of a simple problem prevents the possibility of demonstrating one of the more interesting of the virtues of computer simulation. Often the phenomenon to be simulated is sufficiently complex so that without simulation it is difficult or impossible to anticipate whether the set of principles selected for the program will actually produce the results they are thought adequate to produce. When this is true,

Table 7.1

Computer program for simple learning

```
MAD (03 JAN 1966 VERSION) PROGRAM LISTING ... ... ...
DIMENSION CHOOSE(2), MEAN(2)
INTEGER TRIAL, CORECT, LAST
MEAN(1) = .5
MEAN(2) = .5
START = 0
READ DATA SD, LEARN
PRINT COMMENT $1 RAT LEARNING TO RUN A 'T' MAZE$
PRINT FORMAT $1H − ,S2, H+ PARAMETERS ARE+ ,5,H+
    STANDARD DEVIATION =+, F7.3, H+, LEARNING
    RATE =+, F7.3 °SD, LEARN
READ AND PRINT DATA LAST
READ AND PRINT DATA CORECT
THROUGH NEXT, FOR TRIAL = 1, 1, TRIAL .G. LAST
PRINT FORMAT $H+− TRIAL NUMBER+,13°S, TRIAL
CHOOSE(1) = RANDND.(MEAN(1),SD,START)
CHOOSE(2) = RANDND.(MEAN(2),SD,START)
WHENEVER CHOOSE(1) .G. CHOOSE(2)
PRINT COMMENT $0THE RAT CHOSE SIDE 1$
    WHENEVER CORECT .E. 1
PRINT COMMENT $        CORRECT$
    MEAN(1) = MEAN(1) + LEARN° (1.−MEAN(1))
    END OF CONDITIONAL
OTHERWISE
PRINT COMMENT $0THE RAT CHOSE SIDE 2$
    WHENEVER CORECT .E. 2
PRINT COMMENT $        CORRECT$
    MEAN(2) = MEAN(2) + LEARN° (1.−MEAN(2))
    END OF CONDITIONAL
END OF CONDITIONAL
NEXT    CONTINUE
    END OF PROGRAM
```

the program will sometimes produce something quite unexpected. In this event, ingenuity is often required to determine which part of the program was not needed, or what additional principles are required before the program produces an acceptable simulation of the behavior. In writing a new program, it usually becomes profitable to revise one's thinking about

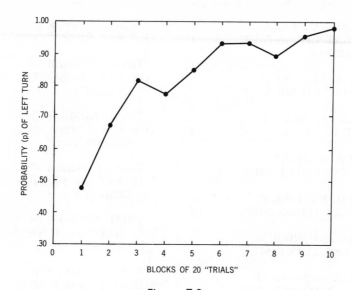

Figure 7.8

A learning curve for four rats learning a T maze problem—as simulated on a computer (see text for explanation).

the nature of the phenomena that are being simulated. The process is rich in potential for producing new formulation and discovery. The computer, with its potentiality for simulation, is neither a substitute for thinking nor a replacement for experimentation, but it can be an important aid in improving both processes.

Table 7.2

RAT LEARNING TO RUN A 'T' MAZE

PARAMETERS ARE STANDARD DEVIATION = .200
                          LEARNING RATE = .015

      LAST = 200*

      CORRECT = 1*

TRIAL NUMBER 1 THE RAT CHOSE SIDE	2	TRIAL NUMBER 3 THE RAT CHOSE SIDE CORRECT	1
TRIAL NUMBER 2 THE RAT CHOSE SIDE CORRECT	1	TRIAL NUMBER 4 THE RAT CHOSE SIDE CORRECT	1

TRIAL NUMBER 5
THE RAT CHOSE SIDE   1
CORRECT

TRIAL NUMBER 6
THE RAT CHOSE SIDE   2

TRIAL NUMBER 7
THE RAT CHOSE SIDE   2

TRIAL NUMBER 8
THE RAT CHOSE SIDE   2

TRIAL NUMBER 9
THE RAT CHOSE SIDE   2

TRIAL NUMBER 10
THE RAT CHOSE SIDE   2

TRIAL NUMBER 11
THE RAT CHOSE SIDE   1
CORRECT

TRIAL NUMBER 12
THE RAT CHOSE SIDE   1
CORRECT

TRIAL NUMBER 13
THE RAT CHOSE SIDE   2

TRIAL NUMBER 14
THE RAT CHOSE SIDE   1
CORRECT

TRIAL NUMBER 15
THE RAT CHOSE SIDE   1
CORRECT

TRIAL NUMBER 16
THE RAT CHOSE SIDE   1
CORRECT

TRIAL NUMBER 17
THE RAT CHOSE SIDE   1
CORRECT

TRIAL NUMBER 18
THE RAT CHOSE SIDE   2

TRIAL NUMBER 19
THE RAT CHOSE SIDE   1
CORRECT

TRIAL NUMBER 20
THE RAT CHOSE SIDE   2

TRIAL NUMBER 51
THE RAT CHOSE SIDE   1
CORRECT

TRIAL NUMBER 52
THE RAT CHOSE SIDE   1
CORRECT

TRIAL NUMBER 53
THE RAT CHOSE SIDE   1
CORRECT

TRIAL NUMBER 54
THE RAT CHOSE SIDE   1
CORRECT

TRIAL NUMBER 55
THE RAT CHOSE SIDE   1
CORRECT

TRIAL NUMBER 56
THE RAT CHOSE SIDE   1
CORRECT

TRIAL NUMBER 57
THE RAT CHOSE SIDE   2

TRIAL NUMBER 58
THE RAT CHOSE SIDE   1
CORRECT

TRIAL NUMBER 59
THE RAT CHOSE SIDE   1
CORRECT

TRIAL NUMBER 60
THE RAT CHOSE SIDE   1
CORRECT

TRIAL NUMBER 91
THE RAT CHOSE SIDE   1
CORRECT

TRIAL NUMBER 92
THE RAT CHOSE SIDE   1
CORRECT

TRIAL NUMBER 93
THE RAT CHOSE SIDE   1
CORRECT

TRIAL NUMBER 94
THE RAT CHOSE SIDE   1
    CORRECT

TRIAL NUMBER 95
THE RAT CHOSE SIDE   1
    CORRECT

TRIAL NUMBER 96
THE RAT CHOSE SIDE   1
    CORRECT

TRIAL NUMBER 97
THE RAT CHOSE SIDE   2

TRIAL NUMBER 98
THE RAT CHOSE SIDE   2

TRIAL NUMBER 99
THE RAT CHOSE SIDE   1
    CORRECT

TRIAL NUMBER 100
THE RAT CHOSE SIDE   1
    CORRECT

TRIAL NUMBER 141
THE RAT CHOSE SIDE   1
    CORRECT

TRIAL NUMBER 142
THE RAT CHOSE SIDE   2

TRIAL NUMBER 143
THE RAT CHOSE SIDE   1
    CORRECT

TRIAL NUMBER 144
THE RAT CHOSE SIDE   1
    CORRECT

TRIAL NUMBER 145
THE RAT CHOSE SIDE   2

TRIAL NUMBER 146
THE RAT CHOSE SIDE   1
    CORRECT

TRIAL NUMBER 147
THE RAT CHOSE SIDE   1
    CORRECT

TRIAL NUMBER 148
THE RAT CHOSE SIDE   1
    CORRECT

TRIAL NUMBER 149
THE RAT CHOSE SIDE   1
    CORRECT

TRIAL NUMBER 150
THE RAT CHOSE SIDE   1
    CORRECT

TRIAL NUMBER 191
THE RAT CHOSE SIDE   1
    CORRECT

TRIAL NUMBER 192
THE RAT CHOSE SIDE   1
    CORRECT

TRIAL NUMBER 193
THE RAT CHOSE SIDE   1
    CORRECT

TRIAL NUMBER 194
THE RAT CHOSE SIDE   1
    CORRECT

TRIAL NUMBER 195
THE RAT CHOSE SIDE   1
    CORRECT

TRIAL NUMBER 196
THE RAT CHOSE SIDE   1
    CORRECT

TRIAL NUMBER 197
THE RAT CHOSE SIDE   1
    CORRECT

TRIAL NUMBER 198
THE RAT CHOSE SIDE   1
    CORRECT

TRIAL NUMBER 199
THE RAT CHOSE SIDE   1
    CORRECT

TRIAL NUMBER 200
THE RAT CHOSE SIDE   1
    CORRECT

REFERENCES

Amsel, A., and Roussel, J.   Motivational properties of frustration: I. Effect on a running response of the addition of frustration to the motivational complex. *J. exp. Psychol.*, 1952, *43*, 363–368.

Amsel, A., and Ward, J. S. Motivational properties of frustration: II Frustration drive stimulus and frustration reduction in learning. *J. exp. Psychol.*, 1954, *48*, 37–47.

Applezweig [Appley], M. H.   Response potential as a function of effort. *J. comp. physiol. Psychol.*, 1951, *44*, 225–235.

Ashida, S.   *Theoretical and experimental analysis of incentive motivation.* Unpublished doctoral dissertation, Univ. Nebraska, 1963.

Baerends, G. P., and Baerends, J. M.   An introduction to the study of ethnology of the cichlid fishes. *Behaviour*, Supplement, 1950, *1*, 1–242.

Bandura, A.   Behavioral modifications through modeling procedures. In L. Krasner and L. P. Ullmann (eds.), *Research in behavior modification.* New York: Holt, 1965.

——————————, and McDonald, F. J.   Influence of social reinforcement and the behavior of models in shaping children's moral judgments. *J. abnorm. soc. Psychol.*, 1963, *67*, 274–281.

Bandura, A., and Walters, R. H. *Social learning and personality development.* New York: Holt, 1964.

Beck, E. C., and Doty, R. W.   Conditioned flexion reflexes acquired during combined catalepsy and de-afferentiation. *J. comp. physiol. Psychol.*, 1957, *50*, 211–216.

Berkun, M. M., Kessen, M. L., and Miller, N. E.   Hunger-reducing effects of food by stomach fistula versus food by mouth measured by a consummatory response. *J. comp. physiol. Psychol.*, 1952, *45*, 550–554.

Berlyne, D. E.   *Conflict, arousal, and curiosity.* New York: McGraw-Hill, 1960.

Bersh, P. J.   The influence of two variables upon the establishment of a secondary reinforcer for operant responses. *J. exp. Psychol.*, 1951, *41*, 62–73.

Birch, D., Burnstein, E., and Clark, R. A.   Response strength as a function of hours of deprivation under a controlled maintenance schedule. *J. comp. physiol. Psychol.*, 1958, *51*, 350–354.

Birch, D., Ison, J. R., and Sperling, S. E. Reversal learning under single stimulus presentation. *J. exp. Psychol.*, 1960, *60*, 36–40.

Black, A. H. The extinction of an avoidance response under curare. *J. comp. physiol. Psychol.*, 1958, *51*, 519–524.

Blackwell, H. R., and Schlosberg, H. Octave generalization, pitch discrimination and loudness thresholds in the white rat. *J. exp. Psychol.*, 1943, *33*, 407–419.

Blum, G. S. *Psychodynamics: The science of unconscious mental forces.* Belmont, Calif.: Wadsworth, 1966.

Bower, G. H., Fowler, H., and Trapold, M. A. Escape learning as a function of the amount of shock reduction. *J. exp. Psychol.*, 1959, *58*, 482–484.

Bower, G. H., and Miller, N. E. Rewarding and punishing effects from stimulating the same place in the rat's brain. *J. comp. physiol. Psychol.*, 1958, *51*, 669–674.

Braun, H. W., and Geiselhart, R. Age differences in the acquisition and extinction of the conditioned eyelid response. *J. exp. Psychol.*, 1959, *57*, 386–388.

Breen, R. A., and McGaugh, J. L. Facilitation of maze learning with posttrial injections of picrotoxin. *J. comp. physiol. Psychol.*, 1961, *54*, 498–501.

Brogden, W. J. Sensory preconditioning. *J. exp. Psychol.*, 1939, *25*, 323–332.

————. Acquisition and extinction of a conditioned avoidance response in dogs. *J. comp. physiol. Psychol.*, 1949, *42*, 296–302.

Brown, J. S., Martin, R. C., and Morrow, M. W. Masochisticlike behavior in the rat: I. Facilitative effects of punishment on resistance to extinction. *J. comp. physiol. Psychol.*, 1964, *57*, 127–133.

Brush, F. R., Brush, E. S., and Solomon, R. L. Traumatic avoidance learning: The effects of CS-US interval with a delayed-conditioning procedure. *J. comp. physiol. Psychol.*, 1955, *48*, 285–293.

Butler, R. A. Discrimination by rhesus monkeys to visual-exploration motivation. *J. comp. physiol. Psychol.*, 1953, *46*, 95–98.

————. Incentive conditions which influence visual exploration. *J. exp. Psychol.*, 1954, *48*, 19–23.

————. The effect of visual deprivation incentives on visual-exploration motivation in monkeys. *J. comp. physiol. Psychol.*, 1957, *50*, 177–179.

————. Discrimination learning by rhesus monkeys to auditory incentives. *J. comp. physiol. Psychol.*, 1957, *50*, 239–241.

Butter, C. M. *Neuropsychology: The study of brain and behavior.* Belmont, Calif.: Brooks/Cole, pending.

————, and Campbell, B. A. Running speed as a function of successive reversals in hunger drive level. *J. comp. physiol. Psychol.*, 1960, *53*, 52–54.

Butter, C. M., and Thomas, D. R. Secondary reinforcement as a function of amount of primary reinforcement. *J. comp. physiol. Psychol.*, 1958, *51*, 346–348.

Campbell, A. A. The interrelations of two measures of conditioning in man. *J. exp. Psychol.*, 1938, 22, 225–243.

———, and Hilgard, E. R. Individual differences in ease of conditioning. *J. exp. Psychol.*, 1936, 19, 561–571.

Campbell, B. A. Effects of water deprivation on random activity. *J. comp. physiol. Psychol.*, 1960, 53, 240–241.

———, and Sheffield, F. D. Relation of random activity to food deprivation. *J. comp. physiol. Psychol.*, 1953, 46, 320–322.

Chambers, R. M. Effects of intravenous glucose injections on learning, general activity, and hunger drive. *J. comp. physiol. Psychol.*, 1956a, 49, 558–564.

———. Some physiological bases for reinforcing properties of reward injections. *J. comp. physiol. Psychol.*, 1956b, 49, 565–568.

Champion, R. A., and Jones, J. E. Forward, backward, and pseudoconditioning of the GSR. *J. exp. Psychol.*, 1961, 62, 58–61.

Church, R. M., Brush, F. R., and Solomon, R. L. Traumatic avoidance learning: The effects of CS-US interval with a delayed-conditioning procedure in a free-responding situation. *J. comp. physiol. Psychol.*, 1956, 49, 301–308.

Coons, E. E., and Miller, N. E. Conflict versus consolidation of memory traces to explain "retrograde amnesia" produced by ECS. *J. comp. physiol. Psychol.*, 1960, 53, 524–531.

Coppock, H. W., and Chambers, R. M. Reinforcement of position preference by automatic intravenous injections of glucose. *J. comp. physiol. Psychol.*, 1954, 47, 355–357.

Coppock, W. J. Pre-extinction in sensory preconditioning. *J. exp. Psychol.*, 1958, 55, 213–219.

Cotton, J. Running time as a function of the amount of food deprivation. *J. exp. Psychol.*, 1953, 46, 188–198.

Crespi, L. P. Quantitative variation of incentive and performance in the white rat. *Amer. J. Psychol.*, 1942, 55, 467–517.

———. Amount of reinforcement and level of performance. *Psychol. Rev.*, 1944, 51, 341–357.

Dinsmoor, J. A. A quantitative comparison of the discriminative and reinforcing functions of the stimulus. *J. exp. Psychol.*, 1950, 40, 458–472.

Dufort, R. H., and Kimble, G. A. Ready signal and the effect of UCS presentations in eyelid conditioning. *J. exp. Psychol.*, 1958, 56, 1–7.

Ehrenfreund, D. Effect of a secondary reinforcing agent in black-white discrimination. *J. comp. physiol. Psychol.*, 1949, 42, 1–5.

Ellen, P., and Feldman, R. S. Generalization of fixation behavior in the rat. *J. comp. physiol. Psychol.*, 1958, 51, 508–512.

Ellson, D. G. Quantitative studies of the interaction of simple habits: I. Recovery from specific and generalized effects of extinction. *J. exp. Psychol.*, 1938, 23, 339–358.

Estes, W. K.   An experimental study of punishment. *Psychol. Monogr.*, 1944, *47*, whole No. 263, p. 40.

——————.   Generalization of secondary reinforcement from the primary drive. *J. comp. physiol. Psychol.*, 1949a, *42*, 286–295.

——————.   A study of motivating conditions necessary for secondary reinforcement. *J. exp. Psychol.*, 1949b, *39*, 306–310.

——————.   The statistical approach to learning theory. In S. Koch (ed.), *Psychology: A study of a science*, Vol. II. New York: McGraw-Hill, 1959.

Ferster, C. B., and Skinner, B. F.   *Schedules of reinforcement.* New York: Appleton-Century-Crofts, 1957.

Fink, J. B., and Patton, R. M.   Decrement in learned drinking response accompanied by changes in several stimulus characteristics. *J. comp. physiol. Psychol.*, 1953, *46*, 23–27.

Fitts, P. M., and Posner, M.   *Human performance.* Belmont, Calif.: Brooks/Cole, 1967.

Forgays, D. G., and Levin, H.   Learning as a function of change of sensory stimulation in food-deprived and food-satiated rats. *J. comp. physiol. Psychol.*, 1958, *51*, 50–54.

——————.   Discrimination and reversal learning as a function of change of sensory stimulation. *J. comp. physiol. Psychol.*, 1959, *52*, 191–194.

Fowler, H., and Miller, N. E.   Facilitation and inhibition of runway performance by hind- and forepaw shock of various intensities. *J. comp. physiol. Psychol.*, 1963, *56*, 801–805.

Fuchs, S. S.   Replication report: An attempt to obtain inhibition with reinforcement. *J. exp. Psychol.*, 1960, *59*, 343–344.

Gerall, A. A., and Woodward, J. K.   Conditioning of the human pupillary dilation response as a function of the CS-UCS interval. *J. exp. Psychol.*, 1958, *55*, 501–507.

Glickman, S. E.   Perseverative neural processes and consolidation of the neural trace. *Psychol. Bull.*, 1961, *58*, 218–233.

Goldstein, M. L.   Acquired drive strength as a joint function of shock intensity and number of acquisition trials. *J. exp. Psychol.*, 1960, *60*, 349–358.

Goodrich, K. P., Ross, L. E., and Wagner, A. R.   Performance in eyelid conditioning following interpolated presentations of the UCS. *J. exp. Psychol.*, 1957, *53*, 214–217.

Gormezano, I., and Moore, J. W.   Effects of instructional set and UCS intensity on the latency, percentage, and form of the eyelid response. *J. exp. Psychol.*, 1962, *63*, 487–494.

Grant, D. A., and Schneider, D. E.   Intensity of the conditioned stimulus and strength of conditioning: II. The conditioned galvanic skin response to an auditory stimulus. *J. exp. Psychol.*, 1949, *39*, 35–40.

Gregg, L. W., and Simon, H. A. Process models and stochastic theories of simple concept formation. *Complex Information Processing*, Paper 85, April 25, 1966, 51.

Grice, G. R. The relation of secondary reinforcement to delayed reward in visual discrimination learning. *J. exp. Psychol.*, 1948, *38*, 1–16.

Guthrie, E. R. *The psychology of learning.* New York: Harper, 1952.

Guttman, N., and Kalish, H. I. Discriminability and stimulus generalization. *J. exp. Psychol.*, 1956, *51*, 79–88.

Hall, J. F., Low, L., and Hanford, P. A comparison of the activity of hungry, thirsty, and satiated rats in the Dashiell checkerboard maze. *J. comp. physiol. Psychol.*, 1960, *53*, 155–158.

Harlow, H. F. The formation of learning sets. *Psychol. Rev.*, 1949, *56*, 51–65.

——————. Learning and satiation of response in intrinsically motivated complex puzzle performance by monkeys. *J. comp. physiol. Psychol.*, 1950, *43*, 289–294.

——————. Learning set and error factor theory. In S. Koch (ed.), *Psychology: A study of a science*, Vol. II. New York: McGraw-Hill, 1959.

——————, Harlow, M. K., and Meyers, D. K. Learning motivated by a manipulation drive. *J. exp. Psychol.*, 1950, *40*, 228–234.

Harris, P., and Nygaard, J. E. Resistance to extinction and number of reinforcements. *Psychol. Rep.*, 1961, *8*, 233–234.

Hartman, T. F., and Grant, D. A. Differential eyelid conditioning as a function of CS-UCS interval. *J. exp. Psychol.*, 1962, *64*, 131–136.

Hays, W. L. *Basic statistics.* Belmont, Calif.: Brooks/Cole, 1967.

Hebb, D. O. *The organization of behavior.* New York: Wiley, 1949.

——————. *A textbook of psychology.* Philadelphia: Saunders, 1958.

Hess, E. H. "Imprinting" in animals. *Sci. Amer.*, 1958, *199*, 81–90.

——————. Imprinting. *Science*, 1959, *130*, 133–141.

——————. Imprinting in birds. *Science*, 1964, *146*, 1128–1139.

Hilgard, E. R. Modification of reflexes and conditioned reactions. *J. gen. Psychol.*, 1933, *9*, 210–215.

——————, and Humphreys, L. G. The effect of supporting and antagonistic voluntary instructions on conditioned discrimination. *J. exp. Psychol.*, 1938, *22*, 291–304.

Hillman, B., Hunter, W. S., and Kimble, G. A. The effect of drive level of maze performance in the white rat. *J. comp. physiol. Psychol.*, 1953, *46*, 87–89.

Hoffeld, D. R., Kendall, S. B., Thompson, R. F., and Brogden, W. J. Effect of amount of preconditioning training upon the magnitude of sensory preconditioning. *J. exp. Psychol.*, 1960, *59*, 198–204.

Hoffeld, D. R., Thompson, R. F., and Brogden, W. J. Effect of stimuli time relations during preconditioning training upon the magnitude of sensory preconditioning. *J. exp. Psychol.*, 1958, *56*, 437–442.

Hovland, C. I. The generalization of conditioned responses: I. The sensory generalization of conditioned responses with varying frequencies of tone. *J. gen. Psychol.*, 1937a, *17*, 125–148.

_____. The generalization of conditioned responses: II. The sensory generalization of conditioned responses with varying intensities of tone. *J. gen. Psychol.*, 1937b, *51*, 279–291.

_____. The generalization of conditioned responses: IV. The effects of varying amounts of reinforcement upon the degree of generalization of conditioned responses. *J. exp. Psychol.*, 1937c, *21*, 261–276.

_____. "Inhibition of reinforcement" and phenomena of experimental extinction. *Proc. nat. Acad. Sci.*, 1939, *22*, 430–433.

Hulicka, I. M., Capehart, J., and Viney, W. The effect of stimulus variation on response probability during extinction. *J. comp. physiol. Psychol.*, 1960, *53*, 79–82.

Hull, C. L. *Principles of behavior.* New York: Appleton-Century-Crofts, 1943.

_____. Establishment of conditioned responses in chick embryos. *J. comp. physiol. Psychol.*, 1949, *42*, 107–117.

_____. *A behavior system.* New Haven: Yale Univ. Press, 1952.

Hunt, E. L. Establishment of conditioned responses in chick embryos. *J. comp. physiol. Psychol.*, 1949, *42*, 107–117.

Ison, J. R. Experimental extinction as a function of the number of reinforcements. *J. exp. Psychol.*, 1962, *64*, 314–317.

Jacobs, B., Jr. Repeated acquisition and extinction of an instrumental avoidance response. *J. comp. physiol. Psychol.*, 1963, *56*, 1017–1021.

Jacobson, A. L. Learning in flatworms and annelids. *Psychol. Bull.*, 1963, *60*, 74–94.

Jenkins, W. O. A temporal gradient of derived reinforcement. *Amer. J. Psychol.*, 1950, *63*, 237–243.

_____, and Stanley, J. C., Jr. Partial reinforcement: A review and critique. *Psychol. Bull.*, 1950, *47*, 193–234.

Kalish, H. I. The relationship between discriminability and generalization: A re-evaluation. *J. exp. Psychol.*, 1958, *55*, 637–644.

Kamin, L. J. Traumatic avoidance learning: The effects of CS-US interval with a trace conditioning procedure. *J. comp. physiol. Psychol.*, 1954, *47*, 65–72.

_____. Retention of an incompletely learned avoidance response: Some further analyses. *J. comp. physiol. Psychol.*, 1963, *56*, 713–718.

Keller, F. S., and Schoenfeld, W. N. *Principles of psychology.* New York: Appleton-Century-Crofts, 1950.

Kellogg, W. N., Scott, V. B., Davis, R. C., and Wolf, I. S. Is movement necessary for learning? *J. comp. Psychol.*, 1940, *29*, 43–74.

Kellogg, W. N., and Walker, E. L. An analysis of the bilateral transfer of conditioning in dogs, in terms of frequency, amplitude, and latency of responses. *J. gen. Psychol.*, 1938, *18*, 253–265.

Kendall, S. B., and Thompson, R. F. Effect of stimulus similarity on sensory preconditioning within a single stimulus dimension. *J. comp. physiol. Psychol.*, 1960, *53*, 439–443.

Kendrick, D. C. Inhibition with reinforcement (conditioned inhibition). *J. exp. Psychol.*, 1958, *56*, 313–318.

Kimble, G. A. *Hilgard and Marquis, Conditioning and learning, revised.* New York: Appleton-Century-Crofts, 1961.

——————, Mann, L. I., and Dufort, R. H. Classical and instrumental eyelid conditioning. *J. exp. Psychol.*, 1955, *49*, 407–417.

Kimble, G. A., and Ost, J. W. P. A conditioned inhibitory process in eyelid conditioning. *J. exp. Psychol.*, 1961, *61*, 150–156.

Kimmel, H. D., and Greene, W. A. Disinhibition in GSR conditioning as a function of the number of CS-UCS trials and temporal location of the novel stimulus. *J. exp. Psychol.*, 1964, *68*, 567–572.

Kimmel, H. D., and Pennypacker, H. S. Differential GSR conditioning as a function of CS-UCS interval. *J. exp. Psychol.*, 1963, *65*, 559–563.

King, R. A. Consolidation of the neural trace in memory: Investigation with one-trial avoidance conditioning and ECS. *J. comp. physiol. Psychol.*, 1965, *59*, 283–284.

Kish, G. B. Avoidance learning to the onset and cessation of conditioned stimulus energy. *J. exp. Psychol.* 1955, *50*, 31–38.

——————, and Barnes, G. W. Reinforcing effects of manipulation in mice. *J. comp. physiol. Psychol.*, 1961, *54*, 713–715.

Kish, G. B., and Baron, A. Satiation of sensory reinforcement. *J. comp. physiol. Psychol.*, 1962, *55*, 1007–1010.

Kohn, M. Satiation of hunger from food injected directly into the stomach versus food ingested. *J. comp. physiol. Psychol.*, 1951, *44*, 412–422.

Lane, H. Control of vocal responding in chickens. *Science*, 1960, *132*, 3418, 37–38.

Lane, H. L., and Bem, D. *A laboratory manual for the control and analysis of behavior.* Belmont, Calif.: Wadsworth, 1965.

Lauer, D. W. *The role of the motor response in learning.* Unpublished doctoral dissertation, Univ. Michigan, 1951.

——————, and Carterette, T. S. Changes in response measures over repeated acquisitions and extinctions of a running habit. *J. comp. physiol. Psychol.*, 1957, *50*, 334–338.

Lauer, D. W., and Estes, W. K. Successive acquisitions and extinctions of a jumping habit in relation to schedule of reinforcement. *J. comp. physiol. Psychol.*, 1955, *48*, 8–13.

Levin, H., and Forgays, D. G. Sensory change as immediate and delayed reinforcement for maze learning. *J. comp. physiol. Psychol.*, 1960, *53*, 194–196.

Lewis, D. J., and Duncan, C. P. Effect of different percentages of money reward on extinction of a lever-pulling response. *J. exp. Psychol.*, 1956, *52*, 23–27.

_____. Expectation and resistance to extinction of a lever-pulling response as a function of percentage of reinforcement and amount of reward. *J. exp. Psychol.*, 1957, *54*, 115–120.

_____. Expectation and resistance to extinction of a lever-pulling response as a function of percentage of reinforcement and number of acquisition trials. *J. exp. Psychol.*, 1958, *55*, 121–128.

Lewis, D. J., and Maher, B. A. Neural consolidation and electroconvulsive shock. *Psychol. Rev.*, 1965, *72*, 225–239.

Lorenz, K. Der Kumpan in der Umwelt des Vogels. *J. Ornithol.*, 1935, *83*, 137–213 and 289–413.

Low, L. A., and Low, H. I. Effects of CS-US interval length upon avoidance responding. *J. comp. physiol. Psychol.*, 1962, *55*, 1059–1061.

Mackintosh, N. J. The effects of overtraining on a reversal and nonreversal shift. *J. comp. physiol. Psychol.*, 1962, *55*, 555–559.

_____. Extinction of a discrimination habit as a function of overtraining. *J. comp. physiol. Psychol.*, 1963, *56*, 842–847.

Maier, N. R. F. *Frustration.* New York: McGraw-Hill, 1949.

Manis, M. *Cognitive processes.* Belmont, Calif.: Wadsworth, 1966.

Marquis, D. P. Can conditioned responses be established in newborn infants? *J. gen. Psychol.*, 1931, *39*, 479–492.

May, M. A. Experimentally acquired drives. *J. exp. Psychol.*, 1948, *38*, 66–67.

McAllister, W. R., and McAllister, D. E. The influence of the ready signal and unpaired UCS presentations on eyelid conditioning. *J. exp. Psychol.*, 1960, *60*, 30–35.

McConnell, J. V. Comparative physiology: Learning in invertebrates. *Ann. Rev. Physiol.*, 1966, *28*, 107–136.

McGaugh, J. L., Westbrook, W. H., and Thomson, C. W. Facilitation of maze learning with posttrial injections of 5-7-diphenyl-1-3-diazadamantan-6-ol (1757 I.S.). *J. comp. physiol. Psychol.*, 1962, *55*, 710–713.

McNeil, E. B. *The concept of human development.* Belmont, Calif.: Wadsworth, 1966.

Melzack, R., and Scott, T. H. The effects of early experience on the response to pain. *J. comp. physiol. Psychol.*, 1957, *50*, 155–161.

Miles, R. C. The relative effectiveness of secondary reinforcers throughout deprivation and habit strength parameters. *J. comp. physiol. Psychol.*, 1956, *49*, 126–130.

_____. Learning in kittens with manipulatory, exploratory, and food incentives. *J. comp. physiol. Psychol.*, 1958, *51*, 39–42.

Miller, N. E. Learnable drives and rewards. In S. S. Stevens (ed.), *Handbook of experimental psychology.* New York: Wiley, 1951.

_____, and Dollard, J. *Social learning and imitation.* New Haven, Conn.: Yale Univ. Press, 1941.

Miller, N. E., and Kessen, M. L. Reward effects of food via stomach fistula compared with those of food via mouth. *J. comp. physiol. Psychol.*, 1952, *45*, 555–564.

Montgomery, K. C. The role of exploratory drive in learning. *J. comp. physiol. Psychol.*, 1954, *47*, 60–64.

Mowrer, O. H. *Learning theory and behavior.* New York: Wiley, 1960.

Noble, M., Gruender, A., and Meyer, D. R. Conditioning in fish *(Mollienisia sp.)* as a function of the interval between CS and US. *J. comp. physiol. Psychol.*, 1959, *52*, 236-239.

North, A. J. Improvement in successive discrimination reversals. *J. comp. physiol. Psychol.*, 1950, *43*, 442–460.

Olds, J. Runway and maze behavior controlled by basomedial forebrain stimulation in the rat. *J. comp. physiol. Psychol.*, 1956, *49*, 507–512.

_____, and Milner, P. Positive reinforcement produced by electrical stimulation of septal area and other regions of the rat brain. *J. comp. physiol. Psychol.*, 1954, *47*, 419–427.

Pavlov, I. P. *Conditioned reflexes* (trans. by G. V. Anrep). London: Oxford Univ. Press, 1927.

Pearlman, C. A., Sharpless, S. K., and Jarvik, M. E. Retrograde amnesia produced by anesthetic and convulsant agents. *J. comp. physiol. Psychol.*, 1961, *54*, 109–112.

Pelkwijk, J. J. Ter, and Tinbergen, N. Eine reizbiologische Analyse einiger Verhaltensweisen von Gasterosteus aculeatus. L. *Zs. Tierpsychol.*, 1937, *1*, 193–204.

Perin, C. T. A quantitative investigation of the delay-of-reinforcement gradient. *J. exp. Psychol.*, 1943a, *32*, 37–51.

_____. The effect of delayed reinforcement upon the differentiation of bar responses in white rats. *J. exp. Psychol.*, 1943b, *32*, 95–109.

Pubols, B. H., Jr. Constant versus variable delay of reinforcement. *J. comp. physiol. Psychol.*, 1962, *55*, 52–56.

Reynolds, B. The acquisition of a trace conditioned response as a function of the magnitude of the stimulus trace. *J. exp. Psychol.*, 1945, *35*, 15–30.

Riesen, A. H. Arrested vision. *Sci. Amer.*, 1950, *183*, 16–19.

Roberts, W. W. Both rewarding and punishing effects from stimulation of posterior hypothalamus of cat with same electrode at same intensity. *J. comp. physiol. Psychol.*, 1958, *51*, 400–407.

Robinson, J. S. The reinforcing effects of response-contingent light increment and decrement in hooded rats. *J. comp. physiol. Psychol.*, 1961, *54*, 470–473.

Ross, L. E. Conditioned fear as a function of CS-UCS and probe stimulus intervals. *J. exp. Psychol.*, 1961, *61*, 265–273.

Schwartz, M. Conditioned-stimulus variable in avoidance learning. *J. exp. Psychol.*, 1958, *55*, 347–351.

Scott, J. P. Critical periods in behavioral development. *Science*, 1962, *138*, 949–958.

Seligman, M. E. P., and Campbell, B. A. Effect of intensity and duration of punishment on extinction of an avoidance response. *J. comp. physiol. Psychol.*, 1965, *59*, 295–297.

Seward, J. P., and Levy, N. Sign learning as a factor in extinction. *J. exp. Psychol.*, 1949, *39*, 660–668.

Sheffield, F. D., and Campbell, B. A. The role of experience in the "spontaneous" activity of hungry rats. *J. comp. physiol. Psychol.*, 1954, *47*, 97–100.

Sheffield, F. D., and Roby, T. B. Reward value of a nonnutritive sweet taste. *J. comp. physiol. Psychol.*, 1950, *43*, 471–481.

Sheffield, F. D., Wulff, J. J., and Backer, R. Reward value of copulation without sex drive reduction. *J. comp. physiol. Psychol.*, 1951, *44*, 3–8.

Shepard, R. N. Approximation to uniform gradients of generalization by monotone transformations of scale. In D. Mostofsky (ed.), *Stimulus generalization*. Stanford, Calif.: Stanford Univ. Press, 1965.

Silver, C. A., and Meyer, D. R. Temporal factors in sensory preconditioning. *J. comp. physiol. Psychol.*, 1954, *47*, 57–59.

Skinner, B. F. *The behavior of organisms.* New York: Appleton-Century-Crofts, 1938.

—————. "Superstition" in pigeons. *J. exp. Psychol.*, 1948, *38*, 168–172.

—————. How to teach animals. *Sci. Amer.*, 1951, *186*, 1–6.

—————. *Science and human behavior.* New York: Macmillan, 1953.

—————. *Cumulative record* (enlarged edition). New York: Appleton-Century-Crofts, 1961.

Spelt, D. K. The conditioning of the human fetus *in utero*. *J. exp. Psychol.*, 1948, *38*, 338–346.

Spence, K. W. The differential response in animals to stimuli varying within a single dimension. *Psychol. Rev.*, 1937, *44*, 430–444.

_____. Learning and performance in eyelid conditioning as a function of intensity of UCS. *J. exp. Psychol.*, 1953, *45*, 57–63.

_____. *Behavior theory and conditioning.* New Haven, Conn.: Yale Univ. Press, 1956.

_____, Bergmann, G., and Lippitt, R. A study of simple learning under irrelevant motivational-reward conditions. *J. exp. Psychol.*, 1950, *40*, 539–551.

Spence, K. W., and Norris, E. B. Eyelid conditioning as a function of the inter-trial interval. *J. exp. Psychol.*, 1950, *40*, 716–720.

Spence, K. W., and Tandler, B. F. Differential eyelid conditioning under equated drive as a function of the reinforcing UCS. *J. exp. Psychol.*, 1963, *65*, 35–38.

Stretch, R. G. A., McGonigle, B., and Rodger, R. S. Serial position-reversal learning in the rat: A preliminary analysis of training criteria. *J. comp. physiol. Psychol.*, 1963, *56*, 719–722.

Thompson, R., and McConnell, J. Classical conditioning in the planarian, *Dugesia dorotocephala. J. comp. physiol. Psychol.*, 1955, *48*, 65–68.

Thompson, W. R., and Heron, W. The effects of stricting early experience on the problem solving capacity of dogs. *Canad. J. Physiol.*, 1954, *8*, 17–31.

Thompson, W. R., and Melzack, R. Early environment. *Sci. Amer.*, 1956, *194*. 38–42.

Tinbergen, N. *The study of instinct.* Oxford: Clarendon Press, 1951.

_____. The curious behavior of the stickleback. *Sci. Amer.*, 1952, *187*, 22–26.

Tolman, E. C. *Purposive behavior in animals and men.* New York: Century, 1932.

Tombaugh, T. N., and Marx, M. H. Effects of ordered and constant sucrose concentrations on nonreinforced performance. *J. exp. Psychol.*, 1965, *69*, 630–636.

Verhave, T. *The experimental analysis of behavior.* New York: Appleton-Century-Crofts, 1966.

Voeks, Virginia. Acquisition of S-R connections: A test of Hull's and Guthrie's theories. *J. exp. Psychol.*, 1954, *47*, 137–147.

Walker, E. L. Variability in extinction scores in Skinner-box problems. *J. comp. physiol. Psychol.*, 1948, *41*, 432–437.

_____. Psychological complexity as a basis for a theory of motivation and choice. In D. Levine (ed.), *Nebraska Symposium on Motivation.* Lincoln, Neb.: Univ. of Nebraska Press, 1964.

_____. *Psychology as a natural and social science.* Belmont, Calif.: Brooks/Cole, pending.

Walter, W. Grey. A machine that learns. *Sci. Amer.*, 1951, *185*, 60–63.

Watson, J. B. The effect of delayed feeding upon learning. *Psychobiology*, 1917, *1*, 51–60.

Weinstock, S. Resistance to extinction of a running response following partial reinforcement under widely spaced trials. *J. comp. physiol. Psychol.*, 1954, *47*, 318–323.

Wickens, D. D., and Cross, H. A. Resistance to extinction as a function of temporal relations during sensory preconditioning. *J. exp. Psychol.*, 1963, *65*, 206–211.

Winnick, W. A., and Hunt, J. McV. The effect of an extra stimulus upon the strength of response during acquisition and extinction. *J. exp. Psychol.*, 1951, *41*, 205–215.

Wright, P. L., Kay, H., and Sime, M. E. The establishment of learning sets in rats. *J. comp. physiol. Psychol.*, 1963, *56*, 200–203.

Yerkes, R. M., and Dodson, J. D. The relation of strength of stimulus to rapidity of habit formation. *J. comp. neurol. Psychol.*, 1908, *18*, 458–482.

Zajonc, R. B. *Social psychology: An experimental approach.* Belmont, Calif.: Wadsworth, 1966.

Hall, J. F., 37
Hanford, P., 37
Harlow, H. F., 79, 91
Harlow, M. K., 91
Harris, P., 32, 67
Hartman, T. F., 52
Hays, W. L., 96
Hebb, D. O., 12, 13, 14
Heron, W., 14
Hess, E. H., 8, 9, 10, 11, 12
Hilgard, E. R., 23, 24
Hillman, B., 24
Hoffeld, D. R., 83
Hovland, C. I., 30, 31, 32, 34, 62,
    63, 64, 66
Hulicka, I. M., 76
Hull, C. L., 24, 27, 31, 62, 65, 68,
    75
Humphreys, L. G., 24
Hunt, E. L., 21
Hunt, J. McV., 35
Hunter, W. S., 24

Ison, J. R., 68, 69, 88

Jacobs, B., Jr., 88
Jacobson, A. L., 21
Jenkins, W. O., 56, 103
Jones, J. E., 52

Kalish, H. I., 64
Kamin, L. J., 52, 53, 54, 58, 59
Keller, F. S., 103
Kellogg, W. N., 23, 85
Kendall, S. B., 83
Kendrick, D. C., 35
Kessen, M. L., 77, 78
Kimble, G. A., 20, 24, 30, 41, 65, 66,
    68, 84, 103
Kimmel, H. D., 35, 52
King, R. A., 59, 60, 61
Kish, G. B., 79, 80
Kohn, M., 77, 78

Lane, H., 104, 105, 122
Lauer, D. W., 85, 87
Levin, H., 79
Levy, N., 85
Lewis, D. J., 61, 101, 102, 103
Lippitt, R., 84
Lorenz, K., 7, 12
Low, H. I., 53

Low, L., 37
Low, L. A., 53

Mackintosh, N. J., 68, 87, 88, 90
Maher, B. A., 61
Maier, N. R. F., 81
Manis, M., 4
Mann, L. I., 84
Marquis, D. P., 21
Martin, R. C., 81
Marx, M. H., 44, 45, 46
May, M. A., 47
McAllister, D. E., 84
McAllister, W. R., 84
McConnell, J. V., 21
McDonald, F. J., 115
McGaugh, J. L., 61
McGonigle, B., 88
McNeil, E. B., 2, 12
Melzack, R., 13, 14, 16
Meyer, D. R., 52, 83
Meyers, D. K., 79
Miles, R. C., 48, 79
Miller, N. E., 50, 56, 61, 77, 78, 80,
    82, 110, 111, 113, 114, 116
Milner, P., 79
Montgomery, K. C., 79
Moore, J. W., 24
Morrow, M. W., 81
Mowrer, O. H., 41

Noble, M., 52
Norris, E. B., 57, 58
North, A. J., 88, 90
Nygaard, J. E., 32, 67

Olds, J., 79

Patton, R. M., 35
Pavlov, I. P., 29, 34, 35, 68, 70, 77
Pearlman, C. A., 61
Pelkwijk, J. J. Ter, 5
Pennypacker, H. S., 52
Perin, C. T., 55
Posner, M., 4
Pubols, B. H., Jr., 79

Reisen, A. H., 2
Reynolds, B., 51
Robinovitz, 135
Robinson, J. S., 79

SUBJECT INDEX